So Help Golf

WHY WE LOVE THE GAME

RICK REILLY

HEADLINE

First published in 2022 by
HACHETTE BOOKS

First published in the UK in 2022 by
HEADLINE PUBLISHING GROUP

1

Cover design by Amanda Kain
Cover photograph © Okea/GettyImages
Cover copyright © 2022 by Hachette Book Group, Inc.

Cataloguing in Publication Data is available from the British Library

Hardback ISBN 978 1 4722 8154 8

Offset in 10.46/16.32 pt Meridien LT Std by Jouve (UK), Milton Keynes

Printed and bound in Great Britain by Clays Ltd, Elcograf S.p.A.

Headline's policy is to use papers that are natural, renewable and recyclable
products and made from wood grown in well-managed forests and other
controlled sources. The logging and manufacturing processes are expected
to conform to the environmental regulations of the country of origin.

HEADLINE PUBLISHING GROUP
An Hachette UK Company
Carmelite House
50 Victoria Embankment
London EC4Y 0DZ

www.headline.co.uk
www.hachette.co.uk

I'd play every day if I could.
It's cheaper than a shrink. —Brent Musburger

Contents

CONTENTS

CONTENTS

CONTENTS

KID

WHEN I WAS ONE, my family was staying at a mountain cabin in Evergreen, Colorado. Apparently, my dad had hit a rough patch with work and we had no place to live, so we stayed in my grandfather's vacation cabin until things turned around.

One day, the radio said a crazed killer had escaped prison. That's the way my brother, John, always told the story later: "A crazed killer." He said Mom locked all the doors and windows, gathered all the knives from the kitchen, got a big pot of water boiling, and stuck the knives in.

My older sister cocked her head at her and finally asked, "Why are you boiling water, Mom?"

"Well, honey," Mom said, "if we're going to stab the man, we don't want him to get an infection, do we?"

Very thoughtful, my mom.

That's about when my dad came back from the car with his weapon of choice—the 3 wood from his golf bag.

The crazed killer never came, but golf became something I grew to fear more than any knife. That's because my dad wasn't just an avid golfer, he was an avid drunk.

You knew when he went off in the morning to play golf, he was going to come home drunk and mean. When he opened the door, we kids scattered. My mom should've, too. He'd yell at her, she'd yell at him, he'd get rough. One time he broke her nose.

Late one night, when I was about nine, he was yelling at her and I got in between to try and protect her. He didn't see me and our feet got tangled and he fell right on top of me. He and I almost never even touched and now, horribly, all his full-grown man 180 pounds were on top of me, all hot boozy breath and Aqua Velva and cigarettes. I vaguely remember my mother screaming and me crying and him laughing, because he was too drunk to get up. I remember running to my room and shoving the dresser up to the door to keep him out.

Whatever golf was doing to him, I hated it. If he was really drunk, he'd forget to take off his spikes and you could hear them clicking on the sidewalk leading to the door. That spikes-on-concrete sound still makes me a little queasy.

One day, when he was out playing golf, Mom gathered us around and told us how to defend ourselves if he ever came at us. Unplug the lamp and hit him, she said. The rolling pin. Lie on your back and don't stop kicking.

My defense was different. I'd try to make everybody laugh, so there'd be no arguing and no fighting and no lamps. The smallest kid in an alcoholic family is the mascot, the little one everybody can giggle at, the one with funny stories and stupid impressions, the one who distracts Dad from braining the rest of us.

On the surface, that worked well. I made a career of telling stories, of making people laugh. But underneath, I was scared and mad and terrified.

I blamed golf for all of it.

———

The Bartender's Son

Once, in a single afternoon at the Irish seaside course Lahinch, *four* people made holes in one on the blind par 3, 155-yard fifth, a practical mathematical impossibility.

Yes, a *blind* par 3. You aim at a white rock that is in line with the pin and pray. If that sounds crazy and antiquated and wonderful, well, get your arse to Lahinch (see page 145).

And so it was on the famous Day of the Four Aces that the Lahinch bar became New Year's Eve in Times Square. They say you could barely get your last free Jameson drank before somebody was offering you another. Word was out around town and the joint was packed with locals, ribs-to-elbow packed. An accordion, fiddle, and banjo were slapping out Irish drinking tunes, and the rosy-cheeked waitresses were getting their rents paid in a single night.

But then, through the front door, came the bartender's wife, holding the ear of her freckled, redheaded seven-year-old son. She marched him up to the bartender and yelled the following into his ear: "Have you any idea what your rascal son did this fine day?"

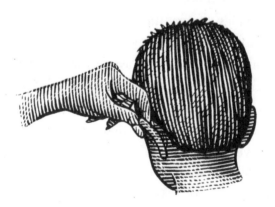

The big bartender was trying to fill 100 drink orders at once, so he said without looking, "What?"

The boy looked at his mother, who nodded. The boy said, "I was puttin' golf balls inta the hole."

3

The bartender pulled his head back, stared at the sheepish boy, then again at his angry wife, all the while starting a Guinness with one hand and making change with the other.

"Well," she yelled, still holding the imp's ear. "Are ya not gonna do sum'tin' about it?"

"Yes," the bartender said. Then he swept the kid up in his arms, kissed him on the forehead, and yelled, "Good lad!"

King of the Playgrounds

The first time you play with Tiger Woods, you can hardly breathe, much less hit a tee shot. For one thing, Woods is much bigger than you think—6-2 with a 32-inch waist and shoulders like a Coke machine. For another, he has a stare that could drill a hole in titanium. For a third, he's Tiger Freaking Woods.

Now, imagine you're barely five feet high, your voice hasn't cracked yet, and it's the first time you've ever played the course. Now imagine it's the first time *anybody* has played the course.

That's what faced 11-year-old Taylor Crozier that day in 2016. A junior golfer, his name was drawn out of a hat to play the very first round at the Playgrounds at Bluejack National, a short family course Tiger had just built near Houston. It would be the first round ever played on it.

Imagine! He and another junior, a girl named Cici, would play an entire round with THE Tiger Woods. True, Tiger had just had surgery, so all he would do was putt, but... whoa.

And now the moment was here. Tiger was leaning on his putter, the ribbon was lying cut on the ground, and all the speakers were finished. It was time. The first hole was an 81-yard downhill par 3 with nothing but heartache behind the green. Cici hit and now it was Taylor's turn.

His uncle/caddy, James Nolen, offered the bag. Taylor put his hand on the 9 iron his uncle had sawed off for him.

"I don't think that's a good idea," his uncle said, reaching for the sand wedge instead. "This is all you need."

The sixth grader stepped up, trying to hear over his knocking knees. Tiger waited.

"There were cameras everywhere," Taylor remembers. "And there was a drone in the air in front of us. And then, having Tiger standing right there. I mean, that was a little nerve-racking."

Gulp...waggle...and...

"Oh, he hit it good," his uncle remembers. "It hit and it bounced..."

...and it bounced...

"I thought it was going to go in the bunker because it hit kind of on the hill," Taylor recalls.

"...but then it started rolling," remembers Uncle James.

...and rolling...toward the pin...

"...and the crowd is getting louder," the uncle recalls, "and it goes in the hole!"

Yep. On the second shot ever hit on Bluejack National, 11-year-old Taylor Crozier made a hole in one. Witness: Eldrick (Tiger) Woods.

Mr. Woods, you need to build harder courses.

"I've never in my life had a sensation go through me like that did," remembers Uncle James, now 70. "The crowd was SO loud. I looked at Taylor, and all the blood just came out of his face. He went white. It just shocked him."

Every eye then went to Tiger, whose hands were on his head, eyes bugged and smile huge. He walked straight at Taylor and yelled, "Are you kidding me right now?" Then he held his arms out and Taylor ran into them for a giant hug.

"He said something like, 'How am I supposed to follow that?'" Taylor remembers.

It just kept getting better. Tiger took the flag off the pin and wanted to sign it for Taylor, but there was nowhere to set it. So he leaned back and signed it on his six-pack abs. Tiger also gave him one of his famous Frank the Tiger headcovers and a signed putter headcover.

One great thing about making an ace with Tiger Woods, it's easy to convince your friends you really did it because there's mountains of video. "Every teacher in every class the next day played it," Taylor recalls. "It was kinda weird watching it. I still didn't believe it."

That was the first ace of his life and he hasn't had one since. In fact, he doesn't play all that much golf anymore. A high schooler now, he's big into baseball and tennis. Can you blame him? After all, when you've made an ace on the first hole of Tiger's course on the day it opens *with* Tiger, what do you do for the second act?

Mini Man

In my secret pact with myself to hate golf, miniature golf didn't count. My dad never played it, so I could. I loved mini golf. When Sister John Agnes was teaching us multiplication tables, I was drawing up mini golf holes in my notebook.

That's why, 50 years later, I decided to try to play as many mini golf holes in one day as one adult human being can stand. Hey, you have your quests, I have mine.

I'll count the score, you count the clowns.

9:01 a.m.—There is only one venue for this mission: Myrtle Beach, South Carolina, the world home of mini golf. If that's not true, then why is it the home of the professional mini golf tour?

Myrtle Beach looks like a five-year-old boy's notion of what a city should be: volcanoes on every block, crashed airplanes everywhere you look, and giant sailing ships bearing the Jolly Roger.

As any right-thinking person would do, I started at Molten Mountain, with its fake blue and pink lava flowing out of giant fake eruptions. I knocked off 36 holes there and saw a sign I've never seen before: "Keep Off the Mulch."

Wait. Isn't it already dead?

10:47 a.m.—It started to hit me that there are no clowns in mini golf anymore. No windmills, either. No castles. Mini golf is much more sedate than it used to be. I blame the lawyers.

And please don't call mini golf "putt-putt." Putt-Putt is a brand name for a nationwide chain of miniature golf courses that were—I hate to say it—way, way better than mini golf. On 1960s Putt-Putt courses of my youth, you actually played *through* all the cool stuff—tiny houses and moving little trains. Your ball would careen through loop-the-loops, around Indy-style metal banks, and over Chinese bridges. Yes, the clown at 18 would swallow your ball, but if you aced it, you'd get a free round. Who's laughing now?

As a kid, one of the best days ever was getting to play the Putt-Putt in Grand Lake, Colorado. There was one hole where you'd putt out and your ball would tumble down a tube onto a turntable, ride it around until it was dumped onto a ramp, zoom down a funnel, get snatched by a tiny golf-ball elevator, and begin climbing to the floor above. To a 10-year-old boy, this was twice as exciting as girls and rockets combined. You'd stalk the staircase next to it, heart in mouth, in case—horrors—your ball would jiggle loose and fall off, causing you to have to start all over. Above, on the second story, you'd thrill to the sight of your ball getting safely dumped out and rolling to a stop, leaving you to sink an 8-footer for your par. We'd only play it 11 or 12 more times before moving on.

Lunch—I wolfed down a possibly ptomaine hot dog from a counter manned by a 78-year-old man. I had to wake him out of a nap just to get it. This was in the middle of year one of the pandemic, which meant all the mini golf jobs formerly held by disaffected, listless teens were now being held by disaffected, listless seniors. This hot dog tasted like it had been there through both regimes.

3:16 p.m.—Finally, I made my way to the Augusta of mini golf, Hawaiian Rumble. It's the home of the mini golf Masters, with a purse of $25,000. They even have a grandstand that holds *at least* 15 people.

My mind did a jig when I thought of the mini Masters. Did the patrons eat mini pimento sandwiches? Was it a tradition smaller than any other? Did the winner don a mini green jacket?

"Yeah, I did get a green jacket," says 2021 champion Rainey Statum. "It's kinda like a Members Only thing." Statum, a Texan, is the major mini man in America today. He wears pleated slacks of every color—purple, red, pea green, forest green, lime green, or pink—with contrasting bowling-style shoes. When you dress like that, you better putt like a witch, and he does.

Statum, a 2 handicap in big golf, averages 5 under in mini golf. He three-putts every six months or so. "I like to lag it up there real soft," he says. "Makes the hole bigger. When you charge everything, it makes the hole smaller."

My advice to you: do not wager with this man on a mini golf course.

5:13 p.m.—I took Statum's advice—lagging everything—at a layout called Spy Glass and had the best mini round of my life— 3 under. Balls kept falling, like drunks into open manholes. Rainey Statum, where have you been my whole life?

7:42 p.m.—Somewhere around bleary-brained hole number 211, at a course called Mayday—with a real-life chopper that had absolutely nothing to do with any hole—I came up with my list of mini gripes.

1. There's no such thing as a par 3 in mini golf. They cannot and should not exist. *Stop putting that on the card just to make people feel better!*

2. If you hit it in the center of three holes and it goes down a PVC pipe to another hole on another green, that ball should go directly into that second hole or else how can the hole possibly be aced? *Stop making that hole!*

3. If you entice us to your course with a real-life smashed car where the doors keep opening and closing, let us play through the doors. *Stop teasing us!*

9:59 p.m.—I putted out at Captain Hook's final hole, my 254th of a very long day. I averaged 39.8 per 18 holes and aced only 1.6 holes per round, which I blame on rocks that do NOT ricochet true. I know 254 isn't divisible by 18, but when you're on a quest and the Crabtrees of Keokuk, Iowa, are *plumb-bobbing* three-footers, well, the top of a man's skull either blows off or he skips a few holes. So sue.

In conclusion, I don't recommend playing 254 mini golf holes in one day or one week or even one month, as the luau music alone will make you lose your ever-loving mind.

Also, stay off the mulch.

Dum Dum

When I was in high school, some guys sprayed their initials on dumpsters. Some threw eggs at houses. I snuck on golf courses.

Par 3s, public, private, cheap, expensive, daytime, nighttime, didn't matter. For me and my buddies, the thrill of sneaking on was even more fun than the golf itself. The best scalp hanging from our golf bags was the very fancy Boulder Country Club. We'd park my crappy Fred Flintstone–mobile (so named because the floorboard was so rusted you could see the pavement going by underneath), walk casually past the mansions, dive between a clump of junipers, jump a wooden fence on 3, play through 8, jump back over the fence, circle down the streets back to 3, and do it again.

That's why I hate the Buhl Park Golf Course in Sharon, Pennsylvania. It's impossible to sneak on.

That's because it's free.

Free as in no charge. Free as in it costs nothing to play. Free as in come on out, play as much as you want, and don't bring your wallet. Where's the thrill in that?

It's actually a lovely little course—nine holes, par 34, no bunkers, lots of trees, well-kept fairways and greens. There's no tee times and there's no locker room and there's no carts. There's no marshal telling you not to play a sixsome, or to hurry up, or not to wear jeans and a *Rick and Morty* tee.

Buhl Park isn't just free, it's been free since 1914, when a rich steel tycoon named Frank Buhl bought 300 acres of land and eventually put in tennis courts, a lake, bicycle paths, a swimming pool, bocce courts, jogging trails, and a golf course, all for his steel factory employees and their families to use, *gratis*. Not only did he build all that, but he put $550,000 in a trust account to pay for all the expenses... forever. With more than 100 years of interest, that'll buy a lot of fertilizer.

The Sharon locals call it Dum Dum because "any regular dum dum can play it." But, actually, it's a genius idea. For more than 100 years, parents have been dropping their kids off in the morning at Dum Dum and picking them up at sunset. Kids play with their friends all day long. You play this game all day long with your friends, you can't help but get good.

"My mom would drop me off and we'd play for six straight hours," says Bob Collins, who is now a teaching pro at the range next door (not free). "I remember she'd give me a quarter and at lunchtime, we'd hide our clubs in the woods and walk to this little bakery shop nearby and get a little peach pie for 15 cents and a pint of lemonade for 10. Man, those pies were soooo good."

How cool is all this? Free golf anytime you want it, two miles from the center of town? And you don't even have to be from town to play it. It's Sharon share alike.

"We think it's the only free golf course in the world," says Tom Roskos, the park director. "We can't find any others like it."

It's such a weird phenomenon—free golf—that people get a

tad confused when they come into the little pro shop. "They ask, 'Don't I have to pay something?'" says Roskos, who spends a lot of his day telling people there's no charge. "They're like, 'But how do I check in? How does this work? It's *really* free? But how? It's so nice!'"

I thought of a catch: with no tee times, there's going to be more fights on the first tee than at a Best Buy Black Friday sale. Turns out there's not. You just park, figure out where you stand in line, and wait your turn, which is usually in no more than three groups. A lot of times, people will ask you to join their group. Makes for a very friendly town.

A lot of smart people say Dum Dum is better than some of the courses in the area that you pay to play.

"That's true," Collins says. "We're lucky to have it."

So, Bob, what would a course as good as Buhl Park charge for a round if it weren't free?

"Oh," he says, thinking for a bit. "I think at *least* $13."

THAT is an outrage.

Miles and Miles and Miles

If you look, golf balls are everywhere. I know two that are sitting right out in the open as we speak and yet nobody *ever* picks them up.

They're on the moon.

If you go up there, they're easy to identify. They're range balls purloined from River Oaks Country Club in Houston. They say "Property of Jack Harden" on them, the old head pro there. One of his members, astronaut Alan Shepard, "borrowed" a couple in

1971, took them to the moon on Apollo 14, hit them "miles and miles," and then just...left.

I remember it vividly as a kid. They might be the two most famous golf shots ever hit, but how they came to be isn't nearly as well known. It started with Bob Hope.

In 1970, Hope was visiting NASA, getting the whole tour, when Shepard noticed that he carried his golf club everywhere. That's when it hit Shepard that the moon would "be a neat place to whack a golf ball."

Of course, there was zero chance of that happening. In a space module, every ounce matters. This isn't Southwest. Bags don't fly free. Apollo 14 had to be light enough to escape the moon's gravitational field and get home. Kind of important. How were they going to let him have a set of clubs and some balls? But Shepard kept thinking it would be a fun way to teach the world about the moon's gravity. Plus, it would be the answer to a trivia question.

Q: Who has traveled the farthest on a buddies' golf trip?
A: Alan Shepard, 240,000 miles.

So, secretly, he took a lunar sampling tool to Harden and asked him if he could somehow attach a club to it. The sampling tool was a 16-ounce aluminum gadget for picking up rocks. It collapsed into five pieces—held together by a string—for easy storage. How was Harden supposed to turn that into a golf club?

An incurable club tinkerer, Harden did. He rigged the head of a Wilson 6 iron to click on to the bottom of the sampler. Took some doing. A few times, when nobody was around, Shepard would put on his full space suit and hit practice shots with it, just to see if it worked.

When Launch Day came, Shepard stored the collapsed club in the module, but how could he get the golf balls aboard without anybody noticing? A: He put them in his socks. The USGA Museum in Liberty Corner, New Jersey, has them in storage. They're white gym socks—the elastic is shot—and they're autographed. But then, name me a museum that *doesn't* have autographed moon socks?

Shepard, then 47, got to the moon and got to work. But when it was time for his final moonwalk, he reached into the utility pocket on his left thigh and produced Harden's space-y 6 iron. He faced the camera and told Houston, "You might recognize what I have in my hand is the handle for the contingency sample return; it just so happens to have a genuine six iron on the bottom of it. In my left hand, I have a little white pellet that's familiar to millions of Americans. I'll drop it down."

He dropped one. But because the suit was so bulky, Shepard had to swing one-handed. The first swing was a whiff. Liftoff aborted.

"Got more dirt than ball," Shepard narrated. "Here we go again."

The second one wasn't much better. It careened sideways two or three feet. "That looked like a slice to me, Al," said the guy in Houston.

Everybody's a critic.

The third try connected and took off low and a little right. Pumped up with a dab of success, Shepard dropped the surprise second ball.

You know how when you're at the range and you're down to your last ball and you want to end on a good one? That was

Shepard right then. He flushed it. As he watched it go, he said, "Miles and miles and miles."

Well, not exactly. Years later, through digital enhancing, it was calculated the first shot went 24 yards. The second went 40.

The man who runs the USGA Museum, Rand Jerris, once talked to Shepard for three hours about it. "What he was amazed at," Jerris recalls, "was how long it hung in the air. He timed it. He said it stayed in the air for 30 seconds."

Shepard wound up moving to Pebble Beach and never hit another ball that hung for 30 seconds. He played in the Crosby Clam Bake and became pals with Bing himself. It was Crosby who got Shepard to give the club to the USGA Museum, where it's on display as we speak.

Alan Shepard, the fifth man on the moon, died of leukemia in 1998. His wife, Louise, died of a heart attack five weeks later, at 5 p.m., the exact time Shepard always called her from the road.

Shepard's moon launches, though, live on. In fact, unless moon men picked them up, the balls are still there. "Technically," wrote Golf Channel's Brandel Chamblee, a friend of the Harden family, "if the balls aren't melted, Jack [Harden] is the only person who owns property on the moon."

TEEN

THE PROBLEM WITH ME hating golf was my big brother, John, made it seem so fun.

He seemed to love golf. He'd tell tales of hitting the range tractor with 5 irons and the metal THWACK it'd make. He'd talk about how awesome Jack Nicklaus was. Jack Nicklaus? I thought. That's Dad's favorite player. What a rat.

Didn't bother John. He got Dad's hand-me-down clubs and he'd chip from the rug onto the couch. He'd play a hole from my dad's bedroom, down the hall, into my mom's bedroom, down the laundry chute, and into the hamper. One day, my dad got a new set of clubs, which meant John got his hand-me-downs, which meant I got my first set of clubs, the hand-me-down hand-me-downs.

By 15, I was playing with John whenever he'd take me. We'd hit any muni where we wouldn't see Dad and play Quarters. What was Quarters? Quarters was anything you could think of.

Me: OK, I won two holes, had three long drives, two up-and-downs, one greeny, two polies, one barky, and I played the whole back nine without losing a ball. That's $3.

John: OK, I won five holes, had four long drives, two up-and-downs, one sandy, one Arnie, two greenys, and a carty—

Me: What's a carty?

John: Par off the cart path. That's four bucks. You owe me a buck.

Quarters was so much fun we never wanted it to end. One time, we played through a brush fire. True. There was a fire on the side of one of the holes and we played down the right side of the fairway, away from it, and kept going. Quarters waits for no fire.

What the hell was happening to me?

A Time to Prey

I'm going to try a first here. I'm going to dictate this piece into my phone as I drive the practice range tractor at the Colorado National Golf Club in Erie, Colorado, home of the University of Colorado golf teams.

What's different about this ball-picker tractor is that it's painted entirely red, with the Nebraska logo on both doors and a Nebraska football helmet stuck to the top. As any Coloradan knows—

...POCK...That one got me on the back left side...

—Nebraska is Colorado's lifelong archenemy. Doesn't matter that they moved to the Big 10 conference. Nebraska could move to the Big 47 and we'd still detest them. So true Buffs fans—even those who don't play golf—come to this range and try to smack it. There's just this sense of—

...THWACK!...OK, that was LOUD. Hit the metal mesh side on the passenger side. I'm going to get out by the 250 sign where it's safer.

OK, that's better. Anyway, where was I?

OK, right...Anybody who's ever played has tried to hit the range tractor. It's as American as drive-through burgers. Even the guy who usually drives this tractor does it. "I feel like it's my duty to hit it," says Nolan Dodson, 20, the range attendant. "Especially when my buddy's driving."

A range tractor is like Evite.com. It's incredibly inviting. This tractor is pushing eight ball pickers out front, tops out at nine miles per hour, and has the turning radius of a Carnival cruise ship. My brother has hit me three times already and my nephew, a college golfer a few years back, at least that many.

The best sniper in town, though, is one of the guys in the pro shop, Aidan Mann, who plays for the University of Wyoming. "I usually take a 4 iron," Mann explains. "You don't need to lead it much, maybe five feet. The best is when you hit them right on the windshield. That scares the hell out of them."

Lovely young man.

Some veteran pickers, like Dodson, make a game of it. After all, a range like this can hold about 5,000 balls, which take about two hours to pick, so you might as well—

CRACK!...OK, holy Jesus, that scared the urine out of me. Hit the top left corner of the windshield. I know who did it, too. The thirtysomething bastard in the blue shirt. He's looking right at me.

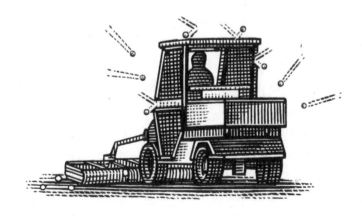

Let's see...OK...Dodson is in this tractor so much, he likes to have some fun with it. "I do whatever I can to make 'em miss," he says. "But I can't do much. I like to see who's trying to hit me and follow the arc of their shots. You know who they are because when they hit you, their arms go up like it's a touchdown. Then, later on, you get out of the tractor and you look at 'em and they go, 'Oh, dude, sorry I hit you.' You know they're lying."

Dodson has been hit three times *outside* the tractor, when he's unplugging one of the scoopers or fixing a knocked-down flag. "They got me in the head once," he said. "That's not pleasant." Range snipers are merciless.

The best place to be a range picker is at the famous Coeur d'Alene, Idaho, golf course. Not only does it have a floating, movable par 3 green, but you hit your range balls into a lake. Yes, you do. The balls surface, then float back to shore on the little waves, where all the picker has to do is scoop them up. Cherry picker gig.

The worst place to be a picker is at World Woods Golf Club in Brooksville, Florida, which might have the best practice range in the world. It's a giant circle, with practice tees on the north, east, south, and west. Everybody hits toward the middle, where there's greens and bunkers to target. Which means the tractor guy is getting pasted from all angles. Like hunting with Dick Cheney, there's nowhere to hide.

But the worst place in *history* was at Rancho Park in LA, where the pickers used to have to strap two Astroturf mats to their bodies, don a construction hat, and do it by *hand*.

...I see the GM is waving me in. I think I know why. Behind me, I can see I've left a serpentine green path through the field of white balls. Just as well. That shot I took on the windshield has made me as jumpy as a fireworks-factory cat...

Now I'm pulling up right in front of Blue-Shirt Guy. I put it in park and get out. I look at him with my best Clint Eastwood squint.

"Hey, you got me pretty good," I snarl. He has a contrite look on his face, like he ran over my poodle.

"Oh, dude, I'm sorry. I didn't mean to. I'm working on my swing. That was a shank 7."

Pah. Likely story.

"Really?" I said. "Let's see your swing."

He showed me.

I believed him.

Xanadu

One day, my brother said, "You know, we could go play Quarters somewhere else."

"Somewhere else?" I asked. "Like...where?"

"Like Denver," he said.

Whoa. The idea that we would leave our little podunk munis and go all the way to *Denver*? To play golf? In the big city? I'd hardly ever seen Denver, much less played golf there.

"Can we?" I said.

"Sure!"

So he called and made us two tee times. "If we're going all the way down there," he reasoned, "we might as well play 36." I was 17 and he was 23, so we took his '56 Ford two-door wagon. The hood didn't close tight and sometimes on the highway it would suddenly fly open, but it was better than my Fairlane I had to park on hills to push start. Besides, who cares? This was my first golf trip.

We started at Willis Case, a scruffy muni west of Denver. It was intoxicating playing *all new holes*. Who knew you could have a par 4 along a highway? We finished, gulped down our hot dogs in the Ford, and made our way west toward Park Hill, which was right in the heart of the city. We got a little lost but eventually found it and the hood never flew up in our faces once.

Oh my god. Park Hill was 10 times as fancy as Willis Case, which made it 25 times as fancy as any place we'd ever played. It had a circular driveway. The clubhouse was huge and stately, with beautiful porches and flowers like some kind of palace.

A little late, we grabbed our clubs and beelined it for the pro shop. "Reilly?" my brother said to the guy behind the counter. "1:20?"

He smiled and looked for the name in his book. Nothing. Page flip forward. Page flip back. Nothing.

"1:20?" the guy said.

"Yeah," John said.

Finally, the guy looked up and smiled. "Well, it doesn't matter. It's really slow today. Go head on out. Enjoy your day."

He went back to his book. I looked at my brother and he looked at me. The guy wasn't asking us for money? He wasn't asking us for…anything? I was about to say something stupid when my brother yanked me by my elbow and quick-stepped it out. We found the first tee box and looked at each other with wide eyes.

"Holy Jesus," I whispered.

"I know," he whispered back. "This place is fantastic."

"This tee box is nicer than our greens!" I said.

"Check out the fairway. It's perfect!"

There were no dead patches, no weedy bunkers, no rutty cart paths. No volcano holes pulled out by drunk greenskeepers.

Everything was green and manicured. Even the chirping of the birds seemed crisper. There was an entire box of free tees and ball marks sitting on the counter of a little starter house there. We filled our pockets, giggling. Had we stumbled on some kind of golf Xanadu?

Giddy, I teed up a driver and hit a line drive, but right down the middle. John teed his up and carved his usual cut into the middle. We threw our bags over our shoulders and practically floated down the fairway.

"There's nobody here!" John said.

"This is crazy!" I said.

But just then, there *was* somebody there. It was the guy from the pro shop, driving a four-man golf cart. He swung up hard into our path, like Mannix fishtailing to stop in front of the bank robbers.

We froze in our tracks.

"Gentlemen," he said. "Do you know where you are?"

We looked at each other.

"Park Hill?" my brother said.

"No," the guy said. "You're at the Denver Country Club."

We just stared at him.

"Are your parents members?"

We shook our heads no.

"Get in the cart."

We were going directly to the parking lot, do not pass Go, do not collect $200. He didn't even let us go get our drives. That really hurt. That was a brand-new Top Flite.

Sixteen years later, I would move my family into a house four blocks from that fairway and join the Denver Country Club. I played that course 500 times when I belonged, but I never got a thrill like the one I got when I didn't.

Why Can't I Be Him?

I'm sick of being happy for Jim Nantz.

I'm sick of how kind he is to perfect strangers, how he always remembers everybody's name, how he's so freaking flawless at his job you want to rip his chest open and look for the hard drive.

I'm sick of him hogging every fun job—the Masters, the Super Bowl, the Final Four, the NFL, the PGA Tour. Can he give somebody else a break? He's already richer than double-fudge cake. His wife is gorgeous. Everything about him just reeks of "I'm humble and nice and I only want the best for you, too" and I'm sick of it. Go somewhere else and be gracious.

I got stuck with him at breakfast the other day in Fort Worth and I accidentally heard his backstory and it's wonderful and sweet and it just made me want to rub half a grapefruit in his nose.

See, when he was a kid, his family would take these annual car trips from New Jersey down to Florida. They'd drop him off at the main entrance of the Doral Open and then go spend the day on a Florida beach, like normal human beings, leaving him an entire day to stalk TV golf announcers, which is the only thing he wanted to be in life.

"The best was if I could see one climbing into one of the towers," Nantz remembers with a smile. "I saw Chris Schenkel do that once. So cool."

On this particular day, his mom had given him a brown-bag lunch—sandwich, chips, and a frozen Coke. But it was hot that day and now the Coke was melting and the bag was a mess and it was only 10 o'clock. So he climbed a tree between 1 and 18 and hid his lunch in the hollow of a branch. When 2 o'clock came, he climbed back up, got the lunch, and ate it while he watched the leaders tee off.

Fast-forward 16 years. Now Nantz is 27 and filling in on the 18th tower for longtime CBS legend Pat Summerall. Just before airtime, he realizes he can see the tree he hid the lunch in. A tingle runs up his back: he's come full circle.

Everybody loves Jim Nantz. And I mean everybody. In 2007, when Bush 43 was president, Queen Elizabeth decided to come to Washington, which meant Bush had to throw a big state dinner. Who did Bush seat next to the queen? Nantz.

"You're here to keep the conversation going," Bush whispered in his ear. Then he sat down, turned to the queen, and said these exact words: "That guy sittin' over there is a longtime friend of the family, Your Majesty. He just did somethin' nobody's ever done in the history of the Yoo-nited States of America. He just did the Super Bowl, the championship basketball game, and the Augusta."

"That's how the president said it," Nantz remembers. " 'The Augusta.' "

Nearly every president has that little "favorite" star next to Nantz's name on their cell phone. When Bush 41 and President Clinton struck up a friendship, they decided they'd like to have a boys' golf weekend out in Maine. They decided to invite Tom Brady and, let's see, who would be the perfect fourth? Yep. Nantz.

You think they talked about the Augusta?

Nantz is such a part of American sports I'm surprised the national anthem doesn't mention him. If you hear that voice behind you at the dry cleaner, you spin immediately. Nantz does the outgoing message on actor Chris O'Donnell's phone. "Hello, friends," Nantz coos. "Chris can't come to the phone right now, but you know that tradition unlike any other—leave a message."

Even that signature "Hello, friends" he uses is impossible to hate. It started in 2002, when his dad was fading away from Alzheimer's. Nantz had to leave for the PGA, but before he left, he said, "Be sure to watch, Dad. I'm going to say a little cryptic message to you on the air, just for you, OK?"

The first words out of his mouth on-air that day were "Hello, friends" in honor of his dad "because my dad had nothing but friends." He's said it every day on the air since.

How are you supposed to compete with this guy?

Here's the worst part. My favorite course in the world is Pebble Beach. The surf, the cliffs, the seals, all of it is so gorgeous you never want to leave. Jim Nantz not only lives at Pebble Beach, he was married on the stunning par 3 seventh.

The sun, the sky, the ocean, it was all the cover of *Brides* as his fiancée, Courtney, walked down a white carpet, where Nantz and 100 friends waited.

"Just as we got to the 'I do's,'" Nantz remembers, "this whole flock of seagulls comes straight up from behind the green and goes flying over us. People actually thought we somehow *trained* the seagulls to do that. I mean, it really was perfect."

Oh, just shut the hell up.

Made for Greatness

When I was a kid, there were no Take Your Son to Work Days. No Daddy and Me Days, either. Eight-year-olds can't get into bars. But one time, out of the blue, my dad took me to something that changed my life.

He invited me to go see Jack Nicklaus, his favorite player.

I didn't want to give my dad the satisfaction, but I'd never seen anybody famous up close, so I went. My plan was to go and then say to myself, *I saw your favorite guy...and I hated him.*

When Nicklaus arrived, my mouth dropped open. He was a Nordic god—windswept blond hair, perfect white teeth, big tan arms. He had a caddy—the first one I'd ever seen—carrying a bag as big as our fridge.

"Ladies and gentlemen," the announcer said. "Please welcome *JackNicklaus!*" That's how he said it. *JackNicklaus.* One word with a capital *N* in it. Like there was only one way to say the name of somebody this cool.

JackNicklaus instantly became my favorite player, too. And over the 40 years I covered him—no matter how well or terribly he played—he never dodged one of my questions, and I've thrown a million at him.

That's how I became the Official Clearinghouse for Things You Might Not Know About *JackNicklaus*, the Greatest Player Who Ever Lived and If You Don't Agree Get Your Own Book.

Here's just 30:

1. When you drive to *JackNicklaus*'s house, you drive a short span on Jack Nicklaus Drive.
2. *JackNicklaus* is shrinking. He used to be 5-11. When I visited his North Palm Beach, Florida, house in spring of 2021, he was 5-7. "Have you grown?" he asked.
3. *JackNicklaus* let me try on his green jacket once. For the picture, he pretended to be the tailor, fitting the hem. But he didn't get that green jacket—his very own green jacket—until 1998. See, every Augusta member gets

a green jacket, but they're not allowed to take it home. They're kept in a cedar closet for their next visit. When somebody wins the Masters for the first time, the staff yanks somebody else's jacket from the closet and puts it on the winner. Then they send him his own freshly sewn jacket in the coming weeks. When Nicklaus won his first Masters in 1963, they got one out of the closet that looked like it might fit. It belonged to former New York governor Thomas "Dewey Defeats Truman" Dewey. But for some reason, they never sent Nicklaus his own jacket. He kept winning Masters and kept getting Dewey's jacket. Geez, what's a guy gotta do? Finally, Nicklaus let it slip to a member that he didn't have his own green jacket, and the next time he came, it was hanging in his locker.

4. *JackNicklaus* has won more at Augusta than anybody in history. Until Tiger, he was the youngest to ever win it (23) and he's still the oldest (46). He was the first to win back-to-back Masters ('65 and '66). He's won the most Masters (six). And in 1995, at age 55 over the course of three days, he knocked in two fairway irons on the fifth hole for eagles. And yet he doesn't have a bridge named after him. Or anything else. Let's get on it, Augusta. I mean, what's a guy gotta do?

5. *JackNicklaus*'s father, Charlie, was such a good athlete that on Saturdays, he'd play fullback for Ohio State and on Sundays, for the professional Portsmouth (Ohio) Spartans, under an assumed name. And no, nobody remembers what it was.

6. If Charlie Nicklaus hadn't broken his ankle so many times playing football and volleyball, we might not ever have

had *JackNicklaus* the golfer. "The doctor said, 'Charlie, if you want to walk the rest of your life you're going to have to give up all this stuff,'" Nicklaus remembers. "That's when he took up golf. But he could only walk one hole at a time and he'd have to rest. I'd be caddying for him and while he rested, I'd hit chip shots and putts and like that. And one day he said to me, 'Jack, would you like to learn this game?'" Jack was 10. Within three years, he was winning state junior tournaments. The first handicap he ever got, at 13, was +3. That same year, he got polio. Lost a lot of weight.

7. *JackNicklaus*'s mother, Helen, rarely played golf. "I remember one of the few times she played," he says, "she shot something like 120. She comes home and she starts going hole by hole with my dad and me. I had to stop her. 'Mom! We don't do that!'"

8. Shy and preferring the background, Helen Nicklaus had one great fear—that her death would cause her son to withdraw from a tournament. She made Jack's sister, Nan, promise that she wouldn't let him pull out of a tournament. Helen died at 91 on the Wednesday of the 2000 PGA Championship at Valhalla, but her son played until he missed the cut on Friday. "I only played for her," he says. That Friday was the last time history's two greatest players—*JackNicklaus* and Tiger Woods—were paired. Nicklaus shot 71 and Woods 67.

9. Helen once turned to her husband and said, "I think our son is made for greatness." She was right. *Sports Illustrated* named him the greatest male golfer of the 20th century.

10. *JackNicklaus* originally wanted to stay an amateur his entire career—like his hero Bobby Jones—so to make money, he sold insurance. In 1960, he was the Junior Agent of the Month for Ohio's Wayne Lewis Insurance Agency. That year, he made about $30,000 a year doing it—about $275,000 today.

11. Speaking of cash, *JackNicklaus* is so loved in England that they printed five-pound notes with his face on them. He carries one in his money clip. It's so frayed it looks like cheesecloth.

12. That money clip, by the way, was his prize for winning a long drive contest in 1963 at the PGA Championship. Using a persimmon driver, he hit a wound ball 341 yards and 17 inches. Like to see Bryson DeChambeau try that.

13. *JackNicklaus* has 18 majors, but he didn't set out to win 18 majors. He didn't even know anybody was counting. It wasn't until the 1970s that "majors" became a thing, mostly because of golf writer Dan Jenkins. "For a long time, I didn't even really point to them," Nicklaus says. Can you imagine how many he might've won if he built his schedule around them, the way players do today? "If Bobby Jones had won 20 majors," he once said, "I would have focused a lot earlier on 20."

14. As of 2021, *JackNicklaus* not only had three more majors than Tiger Woods, but more than triple the seconds (19–6) and five more thirds (9–4). He also played against far stiffer competition than Woods. Unless you think Phil Mickelson (6 majors), Ernie Els (4), and David Duval (1) stack up against Gary Player (9), Tom Watson (8), Arnold Palmer (7), and Lee Trevino (6).

15. In 2000, when Tiger was hotter than the sun, I asked *JackNicklaus* if he thought Tiger would get to 25 majors. "You guys just assume he'll get to 25 or 30," he said. "You just assume he'll never get hurt. Like he won't ever have personal problems. He's going to have kids and a wife. He's going to want to be home more. I'm pulling for him, but he's still got to have a life." He was prescient, except he forgot all the pancake waitresses.

16. Perhaps you forget how many times *JackNicklaus* was left heartbroken at the altar of a major.

    Remember...

    - The '82 US Open at Pebble when Watson chipped in at 17 out of pure prison?
    - The '77 British at Turnberry when Nicklaus shot 65–66 on the weekend and still lost by one to Watson, who played his freckles off?
    - The '72 British at Muirfield when Trevino chipped in from grass thicker than a beehive hairdo? If Trevino hadn't done that, *JackNicklaus* would've owned all four major trophies at once, the way Tiger did in 2000—the Jack Slam.

    Me: Was it lucky?

    "Hell! He hardly even looked at it," Nicklaus says. "He just chopped at it and it plopped perfectly and ran straight into the hole. Bang."

17. The real waste of a major was the '60 US Open at Cherry Hills (won by Arnold Palmer), when Ben Hogan said of Nicklaus: "I played with a kid today who—if he knew how

to win—would have won by several shots." Says Nicklaus, "He was right."

18. *JackNicklaus* used to ride Arnie about that '60 Open. "If I hadn't shot 39 on the back, nobody ever would've heard of you," he'd tell him. Then Arnie would snap back, "If I hadn't three-putted 13 times at Oakmont in '62, nobody woulda ever heard of you."

19. In the '73 British Open, when he was at the peak of his powers, *JackNicklaus* had to play the entire week with a death threat hanging over his head from Patty Hearst's SLA. "They wanted to kill me," he says. "They put a guy named Charlie on me, from [British secret intelligence] MI6, I think. And he slept in my room with me all week."

    How'd you like that?

    "I hated it. I never had a guy sleep next to me for an entire week."

20. *JackNicklaus* considers the '86 Masters his greatest win and the '63 Lytham British Open his worst loss. He loves that Masters because he was given zero chance to win it, hadn't won a major in six years, and his then 24-year-old son, Jackie, was on the bag. And Lytham? "Bogeyed the last two holes. That hurt."

21. *JackNicklaus* doesn't just collect golf trophies. He collects big-game ones, too. He has shot a moose in Alaska, a leopard in Africa, and landed the biggest black marlin in Australia in 1978—1,358 pounds, a fish that took him six hours and 20 minutes to land. Ben Crenshaw, Bruce Lietzke, and Jerry Pate were on the boat with him. The fish put his shoulder in a sling for two days. Six days later, he won his sixth Australian Open.

22. *JackNicklaus* is crazy for paintings of his family and of wildlife. He is not much for modern art, though one time he sat for Andy Warhol, who was supposed to paint two originals and send him one. Except it never showed up. "I've looked all over the world for it," he says. "I've given up."

23. There's a painting of the grandson that Jack and Barbara lost in 2005—Jake, the child of Steve and Krista. Jake drowned at 17 months in a swimming pool while a nanny was distracted. Later that year, Jack was captaining the US Presidents Cup team when his players presented him with the painting. It hangs outside Jack and Barbara's bedroom door. "I almost cry every time I go by it," he says.

24. *JackNicklaus* is a walking box of Kleenex when it comes to kids. He fainted at the hospital all five times his babies were presented to him. He was so nuts about being a father that he promised Barbara to never be gone from his kids longer than two weeks. He and Barbara have lived in the same ranch house since 1970, even though it's probably too small for the five kids when they visit and the platoon of grandkids who come along and, soon, a great-grandchild. "Jack won't move," Barbara says. "He always says, 'We raised the kids here. How can we move?'"

25. One time, at some forgotten event, I introduced *JackNicklaus* to my 10-year-old son Jake. He looked at Jake and then said to me, "Where's Jake's shoes?" Who knew? Apparently, he'd kicked them off somewhere in the arena. *JackNicklaus* helped us look. We found them.

26. *JackNicklaus* and Tiger are 1 and 1A, all-time, on the list of people you'd choose to make a putt if missing it meant you

had to clean up after an elephant parade. "Putting is like free-throw shooting," Nicklaus says. "It's all about concentration and feel." Makes sense. His free-throw percentage on his high school team was 91 percent his sophomore year, 92 percent his junior year, and 93 percent his senior year.

27. *JackNicklaus* has known nearly every president since Eisenhower and played with most of them. His favorite was Gerald Ford, who gave him a puppy from the litter of Ford's dog Liberty.

   "Ford really wasn't bad at golf," he says. "He was about a 13. He'd shoot 84 or 85 just about every time."

   (Which reminds me of the time LPGA great Amy Alcott saw Ford and asked him how he was playing. "Better," he said. "I'm hitting less people.")

28. My dad had a beautiful tenor and *JackNicklaus* has a nice high singing voice, too. There's been a few times when he's sung along to my bad piano playing, leaning on it like Dean Martin.

29. *JackNicklaus* rarely plays golf anymore. His back is a mess. The ball goes nowhere. "When I hit the ball now," he says, "I can hear it land."

30. Standing in his small home office, the walls and shelves covered with every kind of trophy, medal, and honor a golfer can win, I ask: *The house is on fire and you can take only one thing. What do you save?*

   JackNicklaus thought about it, looked around, and pointed to Barbara.

   "Her."

ADDICT

BOULDER, COLORADO, IS A ski town and a yoga town but not much of a golf town. Which explains how I made the junior varsity golf team at Boulder High School with an average score of 95. We were terrible.

Our home course was Flatirons Golf Course. It was as muni as it could be, full of guys with loops in their swings and score clickers on their belts. But Flatirons was where my dad played and I was always petrified I'd see him there, plastered or in a brawl on the seventh hole, but I never did.

The best thing about being on the team was that we got to hit all the balls we wanted. That's when I got hooked on this game. There was no feeling like launching one of those little white rockets so far and high you could stop and watch it fall against the blue of the sky, then the red rocks of the famous Flatirons, and, finally, the green of the trees. One time in 100 I could hit one 250 yards and have it nestle to a stop against the very tree I was aiming at. For a pimply, skinny, troubled kid who'd never had power over anything? It was magical.

And one day there, hitting drivers by myself, deep into this fresh and torrid affair I was having with the game, it hit me. Golf wasn't to blame for the hell in our house.

He was.

This Will Make Your Back Hurt

Next time the spouse says you're playing too much golf, tell them about Bob Gustafson of Bismarck, North Dakota.

From April 1, 2020, to April 1, 2021, Gustafson played 536 rounds of golf, the most of anybody in the United States, according to the USGA.

No fooling—536 rounds in 12 months, in North Dakota, of all places, where 46 inches of snow falls a year and the golf season is shorter than a Kardashian marriage.

"He'll play through almost anything," says Ty Hauglie of Apple Creek Country Club. "Rain, wind. Snow. No problem."

Bob is on the golf course more than a Toro mower. His usual day goes like this:

Up at 6 a.m. Take the two-minute golf-cart ride from his house to the first tee (those two minutes are why he bought the house in the first place). Play nine holes by himself in an hour. Home. Shower. Breakfast. Go to work at the pharmacy he owns with his wife, Lynn. Done at 11:15. Back to the course for 18 at 11:30 with his buddies. Done in three hours, tops. Time for an emergency nine. Breeze through that. Home about 4:30. Relax. Get a bite. Back out with Lynn for 18 more at 6 p.m., since Lynn is nearly as addicted as he is. Done by 8:45. Wait. The North Dakota summer sun isn't sleepy. Why not nine more? There's 63 holes, easy as you please.

When the Gustafsons get home, their dog, Tiger, greets them at the door, Golf Channel is on every TV, and the vacation brochures on the kitchen table are all to golf resorts. He has only one other hobby, barely. One day a year he goes deer hunting. "And even then, I'll be like, 'Oh, man, it's such a beautiful day. I should be playing golf.'" The only thing he doesn't have is an "I'd Rather Be Golfing" bumper sticker.

Bob, one little question ... WTF?

"I don't know," says Gustafson, who is 58 years old and an 8 handicap. "I love golf."

Nooooo.

"I always wonder when I'll get sick of it, but I never do," he says. "It's just the greatest game. It's a great way to be social with your friends. But the best part of it is when you hit that perfect shot, that great shot that just feels so good. That happens once or twice a round. Keeps me coming back."

Bob plays so much golf the staff at Apple Creek got tired of loading and unloading his clubs onto a cart and just gave him one to keep at home. "I think they lose money on me, to be honest," he says.

Ya *think*? Bob pays $3,000 a year for unlimited golf at Apple Creek, plus $900 for the unlimited cart—$3,900 total. Divide that by 536 rounds and it comes out to $7.28 per round, or less than two gallons of golf-cart gas, which Apple Creek also pays for.

You get the feeling if it was announced that a missile was hitting Bismarck in exactly an hour, Bob would get in a quick nine first. Hauglie, the pro, once had to come drag him off the course for his own safety. It was 34 degrees, an inch of snow on the ground, and nearly a blizzard. "And he *still* didn't want to come in," Hauglie says.

Bob saw so much of the last pro, Dave Weiler, that he was the best man at his wedding. He has tons of friends, all of whom play golf.

There's only one problem. In three years, Bob and Lynn are planning to sell the pharmacy and retire.

What will you do then, Bob?

"Play a little golf, I guess."

It's about time.

Golf Nerd Heaven

Maybe your perfect day is loafing on a beach in Tahiti. Maybe it's strolling the streets of Paris. For me, it's rummaging around the Louvre of Golf—USGA headquarters in Liberty Corner, New Jersey.

They're a little sick of me, to be honest, because I take the whole day. The mornings I always spend in the testing center, where people send in ridiculous golf products, hoping the USGA will approve them, which they almost universally don't.

They have a two-faced wedge (NO), a two-faced putter (YES), an incredibly short putter called the Kneel and Pray (NO), a mirrored putter to help you line up (NO), a putter with a piston that fires the ball straight (NO), putters that stand up by themselves (NO), putters with lasers (NO), a pendulum putter (NO), a putter you grip like a divining rod (NO), putters with wheels (NO), and a putter that plays "It's a Small World" upon impact (YES).

They have a rescue club with a built-in weed eater (NO), Japanese tees with plastic backs that wildly increase distance by eliminating spin (NO), tees that lean forward (NO), gloves that are permanently affixed to the club handle for the perfect grip (NO), flagsticks that absorb the impact of the ball and allow it to fall into the hole (NO, *but for the love of God, why not?*), golf shoes that toggle between spiked and spikeless (YES), hats with blinders so you can't look away (NO), hats with a tee hanging off the brim so you can tell if you're swaying (NO), balls that light up on impact (YES), and balls that emit a signal so you can find them (NO FOR NOW).

"Someday," says testing center chief John Spitzer, a former nuclear engineer, "they're going to have little mini drones that follow your ball so you can find it. The military has them now. I think those will be legal because they speed up play."

Yes, please.

They also have the 60-degree wedge Phil Mickelson used to win the Hartford Open in 2001, when he did so many sick things with it people thought it had to be out of Hogwarts. They asked for it. Phil sent it. It was legal.

By the way, did you know...there's no limit of how much loft a club can have? You can have 80 degrees if you want but all you're going to hit is your nose.

At the testing center, I get to watch my favorite show on earth—Iron Rugge (RUG-ee), the golf robot with the perfect swing, smashing balls with drivers all day to test the compression of the balls and the bounce of the drivers. Iron Rugge is the son of Iron Byron, who had to be put to pasture. Iron Rugge has a maximum swing speed of 140 miles per hour because people like Bryson DeChambeau have a swing speed of nearly 120.

They also have a really cool launcher that fires golf balls at a glass wall about 40 feet away. There's a four-foot-by-four-foot window in the wall and the balls fly through it every time and land on the range outside.

Does it ever miss?

"One time," admits engineer Eric Blastic, who runs it, "another engineer was messing around with the tee and left it high and the ball went banging around the rafters, but nobody got hurt."

I can't tell you how badly I want these guys' jobs.

The afternoons I spend in the USGA Museum. They have President Taft's 54-inch driver, the Fishing Pole. (There was no limit on club length back then.) They have JFK's old driver, too, which they showed me while wearing curator gloves. You know how I know JFK was good? The center of the face was nicely worn out. Oh, and on a high shelf, they have Ronald Reagan's old golf bag, right next to John Daly's.

They have the actual scorecard from the day a 20-year-old sporting goods clerk named Francis Ouimet (pronounced WE-MET) shocked two of the greatest golfers in the world—Harry Vardon and Ted Ray—to win the 1913 US Open. Did you know...the score that day was kept by British golf writer Bernard Darwin, Charles Darwin's grandson?

(The only guy I know who's more nuts about Ouimet than me is Ben Crenshaw. He was the Ryder Cup captain in 1999 at Brookline. I was standing near him when Justin Leonard stunned the Euros by holing that 45-foot putt to win the Cup on the 17th hole, not even a lob wedge from Ouimet's boyhood bedroom. Crenshaw was running around in a panic, eyes big as fishbowls. He grabbed me by the shoulders and yelled, "On Francis's hole, Rick! On Francis's hole!")

They have Ben Hogan's first trophy—a little silver golfer on a stand, maybe four inches high, which he won at 15 in Fort Worth at the Glen Garden Country Club Christmas caddy tournament. Did you know...one of the caddies he beat that day was Byron Nelson?

Did you know . . . Bobby Jones's famous Calamity Jane putter, the one he used to win the Grand Slam in 1930 and a few dozen other tournaments, was badly split down the shaft? That's why Jones had all that famous black tape on it.

Lastly...(they're kicking me out)...did you know...the most underrated athlete in American history, Babe Didrikson Zaharias, won the 1954 US Open by 12 shots while wearing a colostomy bag? It was fallout from her cancer surgery the year before. Nobody knew. She hid it under her skirt that whole week.

(OK, that's maybe the only thing I'm glad they *don't* have.)

What's This Putter Thing Do?

Lucas Glover is a funny southern dude who reads two books a week. He's yes-sir polite, humble, and pays his caddy right. So how come God hates him?

Look, pro golf can be a nasty way to make a living. You can lose your swing, your confidence, your backers. You can get the hideous hooks and the unspeakable slices. Your putter can stop speaking to you entirely. If the travel doesn't break you down, it will break down your wife. You don't see your kids, your friends, your future. Every fairway can start to look like a sidewalk, every green like a tea saucer. Your knee can go out, your back, your mind.

By the time he was 40, nearly all of these things had happened to Lucas Glover.

It all started well enough. A Clemson All-American, he'd won three times on Tour by the time he was 32, including his masterpiece, the 2009 US Open at Bethpage Black, a course that is harder than climbing Everest in flip-flops. He rose to 15th in the world golf rankings.

Then he drove his parade straight off a pier. After years of perfectly wonderful golf, he couldn't sink a two-foot putt. If you Google "worst putt in golf history," a Glover putt comes up. It can't be more than 18 inches. (Warning: it's painful to watch.) The irony is that putt was for a 60. It was like a marathon runner wiping out the field and then bouncing backward off the finish-line tape. Everybody knew it: Lucas Glover had the dreaded yips.

"They're mini panic attacks," Glover says. "It's a complete loss of motor skills. I literally have the putter in my hand and can't remember what to do with it. It'd be like if you were driving and you suddenly didn't know how the steering wheel works."

We golfers won't even say the y-word out loud. The yips nearly wrecked Tom Watson. I was friendly with the late oil tycoon Jack Vickers. He got them so bad he had to putt facing *away* from the hole and backslap it. After one of his surgeries, no less than Tiger Woods got a case of the chip yips so bad that he was chipping *around* greenside bunkers.

"It never happens on the long ones, just the short ones," Glover says. "It's a stigma. And I never know when it's going to hit me. I'll always have them. It's just that now I have ways to deal with them."

So how does he deal with them? He putts short ones with his eyes closed. "I haven't hit a short putt on Tour with my eyes open in four or five years. Nobody ever seems to notice."

Wait. What?

"Yeah, closing your eyes keeps you from knowing where the ball is. You can't flinch at the moment of impact if you don't know when the moment will be."

Then there was his marriage.

During the Players Championship in 2018, police were called

to the house Glover was renting when his wife, Krista, called 911 and reported that Lucas's mother was attacking her. That's when Lucas grabbed the phone.

Lucas: Hello?

911 Operator: Yes, hello. Who's this?

Lucas: This is the supposedly sane one of the bunch...My wife is trying to blame it on my mother, which is not the case at all. My mother is the one who's blameless. My wife is just going crazy.

911 Operator: Can I talk to your wife?

Lucas: No, you cannot...When the deputies get here they need to talk to the male, that would be me, because these other two are out of their minds.

The deputies came, talked to everybody, and filed a report saying Krista hadn't attacked just his mom, she'd "forcefully attacked" and "injured" Lucas. That started all kinds of talk that Glover was married to a husband beater. Krista was charged with domestic violence and resisting arrest but Glover has insisted a hundred times over that she never hit him. Things are better now, he says. "We did some things because we needed to," he says. Whatever that was, it worked. They're still married.

Then there was the sudden reappearance of his birth father.

Ron Musselman was a relief pitcher back in the day for the Seattle Mariners and the Toronto Blue Jays. He separated from Lucas's mom when Lucas was a toddler, fell behind on child support, and wound up being banned from seeing his son until Lucas turned 18. At 12, Lucas was officially adopted by his stepdad,

Jim Glover, and renounced his birth father. "I made a choice as a kid, to delete that chapter as best I could from my life."

That worked until not long ago, when Musselman showed up at a tournament in Mexico. "This guy stepped into the crosswalk in front of me and I was like, 'Hey, I think I know that guy.' He said hello. I said hello. I hadn't seen him in 23 or 24 years. He didn't want anything. And I expect I won't see him for quite a while."

All this crap makes it really hard on a guy to make cuts, much less win. Glover stopped doing much of either. He nearly lost his card twice. He missed eight straight US Open cuts. By the time he turned 40 in late 2019, he'd gone eight straight years without a win.

And yet, through all of it, golf's Job has kept his manners and smile and good cheer. I have no idea how. The game was screaming at him to quit and Glover wouldn't listen. I admire that about him. I admire that about people in golf who could quit, probably should quit, really *need* to quit, but don't.

Which is why it was so wonderful that after 10 straight years of "Aw, you'll get 'em next time, man" Glover birdied five of the last seven holes and won the 2021 John Deere Classic.

"I never once thought about hangin' them up," Glover says. "I always believed. I knew I was good enough. Besides, what the heck else was I gonna do that's as much fun as this?"

Maybe he *is* the sane one.

The Great Escape

The balls were made of boot leather. The holes were tree stumps. Out-of-bounds was the fence of a German POW camp—double barbed wire 20 feet high. The hazards were the machine guns of the guards in the towers.

The year was 1943 and the place was Stalag Luft 3—160 miles southeast of Berlin. That's when a ladies mashie golf club turned up out of nowhere and sparked the most unusual course in golf history.

The camp was for captured American and British aviators, among them an Englishman named Pat Ward-Thomas, who couldn't believe his eyes when he saw the mashie. "I seized on it like a starved dog would seize a bone," wrote Ward-Thomas, who would go on to be a renowned British golf writer.

But what good is a club without a ball? Ward-Thomas took a lump of wood and wrapped yards of string around it, covered by some cloth. It was awful, but he and his buddy took turns chipping that ball back and forth for hours in the dirt between their barracks.

The rest of the 800 POWs saw it and got jealous. They began fashioning their own balls. Some covered theirs in sticky bandages purloined from the infirmary. Some would take razors and shave the rubber off the heels of their boots for the core, then cover them in more rubber from their shoes. I've seen two of these balls at the USGA Museum. They look like leather hacky sacks.

But what good is a club and a ball without a hole? So... "We designed a course," Ward-Thomas wrote for *Sports Illustrated* 26 years later, "using doors, tree stumps, and telephone poles for holes." Sand greens were lovingly built and tended by prisoners. Soon, they had a nine-hole par 3 course, measuring about 900 yards, with the longest hole being 150 yards. Soon everybody wanted a tee time at Stalag Luft 3.

But what good is a tee time when there is only one club? It's not that guys didn't try to build others. Shafts were made from hockey sticks whittled down with the one knife they'd stolen. Club heads were fashioned from melted-down metal water jugs. Some took stovepipes out of their rooms and tried to make irons.

Finally, somebody wrote to the Red Cross asking for a few more clubs. That must've puzzled the mail room there. How exactly were golf clubs going to help POWs? Over-club a few guards? The Red Cross sent them anyway, and golf got so big at Stalag Luft 3 that different "country clubs" were formed and matches held.

There were hazards, of course, like getting shot looking for your ball. "Inside the double barbed-wire fence surrounding the camp was a low rail," Ward-Thomas wrote, "leaving a no-man's-land of some 10 yards width. If you stepped in this, you could be shot."

For some reason, the guards showed mercy. Maybe it's because many of them had been aviators themselves. Maybe it's because many were old, since any able-bodied German was fighting the war. The guards gave the golfers white coats to wear when they needed to go into no-man's-land to retrieve balls. If a ball sailed over the outer fence, though, *auf Wiedersehen.* "There was nothing for it but to wait for a passerby...to throw it back," Ward-Thomas wrote.

The best thing about the links of Stalag Luft 3, though, had nothing to do with golf at all. It helped give cover for the daring escape the rest of the camp was hatching. Underneath the very feet of the wildly enthusiastic and noisy golfers, dozens of men were at work 24/7 digging the famous Tom, Dick, and Harry tunnels, the inspiration for the movie *The Great Escape.*

Seventy-six men got away through those tunnels. Whether you're talking bunkers or prisons, that's a very good out.

The Jordan Rules

Some people are born to compete. Some are born to win. Michael Jordan was born to compete, win, leave you lying on the curb half-dead, get his Ferrari and drive it over your legs, then back up and do it again.

Just because you don't see Jordan on your TV set much anymore doesn't mean he isn't still a killer. The lion doesn't just suddenly give up meat.

I've never played golf with Jordan, but he played through me and baseball star Steve Garvey once in San Diego. It was a blind par 5 and Jordan's second shot trundled up and came to rest on the green. Garvey put it on a tee. When Jordan came along, he was not exactly chatty. Over the years, I've probably asked 50 people what it's like to play golf with the man. The answers are so uniform that I've formulated the Jordan Rules. If he ever asks you to play with him, follow these rules or God help you.

1. There's NO 18 holes. There's NO 27. There's ONLY 36. "Michael Jordan plays 36 holes pretty much every day of his life," says Tour star Keegan Bradley. "No joke." On the day the 1992 US men's Olympic basketball team crushed Puerto Rico, Jordan played 36 holes. There's a simple reason Jordan loves golf so much. Unlike basketball, there are no teammates to let him down.

2. On the way to 36, there's NO stopping at the end of the first 18 for "drinks" or "snacks." Stopping is for pussies.

If you're thirsty at the custom-built golf course Jordan owns—Grove XXIII in Florida—your beer will be delivered by drone. He's not called Air Jordan for nothing.

3. You can play for $1. You can play for $100,000. Jordan doesn't care. He will try to separate you from all you hold dear. One of his buddies told me: "Michael gets the biggest kick out of cocky guys who meet him for the first time and go, 'OK, Michael, I'll play you $10,000 a hole.' He's like, 'Oh, man. Am I supposed to be scared?' This is a guy who's had putts for $1 million."

4. If you try to stand up to Jordan by pressing or doubling the bet, he grins and says, "Kids who play in the street end up getting hit." Usually, what gets hit is your 401(k).

5. Jordan does NOT play without a bet, ever. Yes, you might be playing this hole for $50,000, with $10,000 skins, but if you both have the same length putt, he will want something extra on them. He'll extract the cigar from his teeth and go, "We got somethin' on these putts?" And there'd BETTER be somethin' on these putts.

6. Do NOT putt Jordan for money. Jordan's short game—especially his chipping, bunker game, and putting—is terrific. He has the hands of a mohel. "From 100 yards in," says a pro who asked me not to print his name, "that dude is nearly Tour quality." You know a guy is scary when you don't want your name attached to a *compliment*.

7. Do NOT bet Jordan at all, but if you must, bet him on whose drive will hit the fairway. Jordan sprays his driver like a Rain Bird.

8. Do NOT bet Jordan, but if you must, do NOT do it at Grove XXIII. The pros who belong there—Rickie Fowler, Justin Thomas, Phil Mickelson—call it "Slaughterhouse XXIII," because Jordan is nearly impossible to beat there. It's his course so it's tailored to the exact distances he hits his driver. "The longer you hit it, the tighter the fairway gets," Fowler told the excellent golf podcast *Subpar*. Fowler has to give Jordan 10 shots. "If I'm giving him a shot, I have to hit my driver into some really small spots."

9. Do NOT give Jordan shots. He hits wedges like dart pros hit triple 20s. "If I'm giving him a shot and he's on in two," Fowler explained, "I've got no shot. I've got to play completely nuts to beat him."

10. You can play in a T-shirt (Jordan does). You can get a free cigar from the in-house cigar roller (Jordan starts smoking them at 8 a.m.). Hell, you can have an Air Jordan–shaped ice cube in your bourbon. But you MUST keep up. There are no governors on the carts, which can go 35 mph. Step on it. If you're not done with 36 holes in four hours, he'll take it out on you in cards afterward. You do NOT want that.

I raise you for your house.
Gulp.

Air Ball

In all his 36 years as a club pro, Dave Podas has seen people play with all kinds of clubs—new clubs, old clubs, rental clubs, sawed-off clubs, even hickory clubs.

But until this moment, he'd never seen someone play with *no* clubs.

It happened in 1999 at East Lake Golf Club, near Atlanta. He was to play a practice round with Stephen Ames, who would later become famous for challenging Tiger Woods and getting beat 9 and 8 for his trouble. Podas had never met Ames, but they'd signed up for the same tee time to get one last practice round in before US Open qualifying began.

The two shook hands and Podas stepped to the tee and hit his drive down the middle. Now it was Ames's turn. He stepped up and took his stance but he didn't put a tee in the ground. Or a golf ball on top of it. Or even bring a golf club with him. No tee, no ball, no club. Still, he took his stance and waggled an imaginary club and picked out an imaginary line and stared at an imaginary ball.

Podas looked at Ames's caddy, who had a full set of clubs, none of which were being used. Ames waggled again and made a beautiful swing, but *sans* driver. Podas looked at his own caddy, who looked right back at him. *What in the Jesus...?*

Ames posed over his imaginary drive, staring into the sky at...what?...and then began striding down the fairway. Podas stood there, scratching his head. He's a shy Minnesota guy and

Ames had done all this with pure confidence, as though he did it daily, so Podas didn't ask. Maybe Ames had just won the Marcel Marceau Invitational?

In the middle of the first fairway, Podas came to his ball, took a 9 iron, and hit it on the green. Ames watched it fly, said, "Good shot," and then walked another 10 yards forward, stopped, set up over the invisible golf ball, waggled, and took a swing. Again: no club. Ames's caddy stood next to him, a set of perfectly good golf clubs on his shoulder, a bag full of balls and tees in the pouch, all unused.

Again, Ames posed a little as he watched his "shot" fly and then walked on toward the green. No club, no ball, no divot, no comment. Podas made a face at his caddy and his caddy made a face at him. *Are we missing something...?*

The same thing on 2. Ames made nice swings. Good tempo and good balance, just no golf club. Podas made his par, which was matched by Ames's par that nobody could see but him.

Was Podas on Punk'd? Finally, on the third tee, Podas couldn't take it anymore.

"All right, Stephen," he said. "What the *hell* are you doing?"

Ames turned to him. "Well," he said. "I don't want to tire myself for tomorrow. So I'm just going over where I'll be on each hole, mapping it out, seeing what it'll look like."

"Craziest thing I've ever seen," Podas recalls.

Finally, on the 18th green, the two players finished, Podas having used a Titleist Pro V1 and Ames his imagination. They shook hands and wished each other good luck and started to walk off in opposite directions.

And that's when Podas's caddy stopped and hollered to Ames. "Hey, man," he yelled. "What'd you shoot?"

WRITER

WHEN I WON THE state high school sportswriting contest, I found out who judged it. He was an editor for our town paper, the Boulder Daily Camera. By sheer luck, I worked next to his wife that summer as a bank teller. I annoyed her so relentlessly that her husband finally called me and gave me a part-time job taking phoned-in high school scores at night.

One day, they told me to go cover the Colorado Open golf tournament. Oh my god. I was going to be talking to actual professional golfers. Could it be long before I was writing about my hero, Jack Nicklaus?

But it was a golfer I'd never heard of who changed my life that day. His name was Larry Mowry, a journeyman who'd climbed to the top of the leaderboard. I was in a scrum with a couple of gnarled Denver sportswriters when he said, "Boys, putting is so much easier when you don't have the shakes."

They laughed and scribbled it down, but I didn't get it.

"What do you mean?" I said.

The three of them looked at me like I'd said something in Swahili. Mowry smiled and said, "I'm a recovering alcoholic. I used to drink like a fish every single night and then wake up and try to play golf. My hands would literally shake over a putt. Some mornings, I'd still be drunk. It's easier now I don't have to figure out which of the three balls is mine."

The other two laughed again and wrote it down. But I just stared at Mowry. Something emotional smacked me. Here was a golf drunk who'd stopped? Why couldn't I have a dad like Larry Mowry? I nearly started bawling. I had to walk away.

That's when I realized three things. (1) There were good men in the world. (2) Writing about golf was really just writing about people who happened to play golf. And (3) that meant there were stories everywhere.

———————

Rabbit Run

When some guys miss a cut on Tour, they go straight to the bar and knock back some Forget Juice. Or they go beat balls on the range until they blister. Or they call their mental coach.

Not Ricky Meissner. When he missed a cut, he'd go rob a bank.

Meissner was a star junior from Silver Springs, Maryland. Big and long, he won the 1962 Schoolboy Championship in his home state. He was a kid with a whole lot of giant novelty checks in his future. But Vietnam soon raged, so the son of a police officer did his part by joining the Marines. When he got out, he wasn't nearly the player he'd been.

Still, his dream was to play the Tour and he wasn't giving it up. He got good enough again to make the 1970 and 1974 US Opens, though he missed the cut at both. He became a Tour rabbit, one of the hundreds of guys each week who would try to Monday qualify for the few spots available.

In those days, being a rabbit was an easy way to get stomped. Meissner was traversing the country in a beat-up borrowed van and cooking his dinners at campsites on a portable hibachi grill. He was nearly broke. One day, he went to the bank to take out a $20 bill when his eye was drawn to the teller's drawer. Something toggled in his brain.

The next day, he went into a bank with a .32 automatic under his sweater. He flashed it to the teller and quietly told her to fill his vinyl briefcase with the cash. He walked out with $2,600.

"I told myself I'd do this one and that would be it," Meissner once said, "but I was wrong. One led to two and that led to others. Once I'd fail to qualify on Monday, I'd drive around town, look for a bank to hit, hit it, then drive on to wherever I had to play the following week."

Pretty soon he wasn't driving the beat-up van anymore. He was driving a new Cadillac. And no more campgrounds. He was staying in nice hotels. He was even helping other rabbits out with a little lettuce now and then. He became a kind of Robin Hood in plaid pants.

Getting ready to knock over a bank, though, made him sick to his stomach. He'd get diarrhea. He'd swear this was the last one. Then he'd put fake plates on the Cadillac, dye his hair black, glue on a mustache, screw up his courage, and go.

One time, a teller freaked out. "Oh, God, no!" she wept. "Please no!"

"Relax," Meissner whispered. "Nobody's going to get hurt here."

"No! No! Please!" she whimpered.

"Lady," he assured her. "It's not even loaded." He showed her the empty chambers. She reached into the drawer and gave him the cash.

Newspapers started calling him The Gentleman Bandit. He was a gentleman with the loot, too. Once, he came upon an elderly Georgia couple on their way to Disney World. Their car had broken down. "They were so upset," Meissner remembered. "Their vacation was ruined." He drove them to a local dealership and bought them a station wagon, right off the showroom floor, for $8,400. He handed them another $1,600 cash so they could have fun in the Happiest Place on Earth.

Meissner had no guilt about it. The banks were backed by the government, he figured, and this is what the government deserved. He'd been a national-class young player and lost all those years to their stupid war. They'd robbed his dream, so he'd rob their banks. Besides, it wouldn't be long. He'd turn one of his rabbit spots into a big check, which would put him on the money list and get him his Tour card, and all this would be over.

That chance came at the 1977 Tallahassee Open. He qualified, then shot a 68 on the first day, good enough for the lead after the first day. Imagine that: a wanted bank robber was beating Tour stars like Hubie Green and Ed Sneed, and on national television no less. After years of stiffing him, had fate finally cuddled up to Ricky Meissner?

Nope. It all came apart like wet Kleenex. The next three days he shot 74–77–81 and made almost nothing. Banks would have to pay for this. He went on a bender.

From June of 1977 to June of 1978, Meissner robbed 19 banks, almost all of them the week of PGA Tour stops. If there had only been an FBI agent who'd been a golf fan...

Wait a second. Tucson? Milwaukee? Fort Worth? These are all golf cities!

Finally, Meissner got sloppy. He robbed a bank in Maryland without changing his license plates. Somebody wrote them down as he was driving away. When the FBI cuffed him, he didn't have a dime. He'd spent it all paying for his golf, supporting his family back home, and buying gifts for perfect strangers. He got 25 years.

But Ricky Meissner did make golf history as the only pro to ever lead the Tour in money while making only one cut.

The Cheeseburger Ruling

The 1970s superstar Tom Weiskopf, now a strict tea sipper, was once a rogue whose elbows polished more bars than a case of Pledge.

Early one Friday morning at the Utah Open, Weiskopf arrived at the first tee having not seen a bed the night before, much less slept in one. He'd gone from an 80-proof night with the iron-livered writer Dan Jenkins straight to a tee time only fit for roosters. "I'm not sure I even got my shoes tied," he remembers.

On the third hole, he split the middle of the fairway with his tee shot and then announced to his playing partners he needed a ruling.

"A ruling?" one said. "From the middle of the fairway?"

"Right away," Weiskopf growled.

When the rules official trundled up in his cart, he looked at Weiskopf's ball and then at Weiskopf. He had the same expression you used to see on the RCA dog.

"Tom," the rules guy said, "what possible ruling could you need?"

Weiskopf leaned on the cart roof with both hands. "I am hungover as *hell*," he said. "I need two cheeseburgers, two chocolate shakes, and four aspirin in the next 15 minutes or I'm withdrawing."

The rules guy looked at Tom's bloodshot eyes and peeled off, probably because Weiskopf was the biggest name in the tournament and right in the hunt besides. Weiskopf waited on his "ruling" and waved two groups through. Soon, he had his gooey breakfast, his soul-replenishing ice cream, and his pills. He gobbled all that down, then proceeded to birdie 8 of the next 14 holes.

Hundreds of yards away, Jenkins was watching the eighth birdie go up on the scoreboard. He looked at it and said, "Greatest round of golf a dead man walking ever played."

What Won't Phil Do?

I'm a Phil Mickelson guy, not a Tiger Woods guy, and here's why: Phil lets us into his life. Tiger stations Dobermans at the door of his.

It doesn't matter what's happening in Phil's life, whether wife Amy is about to give birth at the same time he's trying to win his first major, or his mom is fighting cancer, or he's just been diagnosed with arthritis, he's always as open as a brand-new Safeway.

I've been to his house. I have his number. I've had 50 one-on-ones with him. I've never been to Tiger's house. I don't have his number. I haven't had a one-on-one with him since 1997. Tiger's thoughts are on a need-to-know basis, and nobody needs to know. Phil practically gives you the passkey to his mind.

And what a mind it is. Phil Mickelson is easily the most fascinating athlete I've ever covered. Every golfer goes to teachers to get better. Phil goes to scientists. Remember the constant chewing of gum to "help me release nervous tension"? Remember the three deep meditative breaths before every shot at his Kiawah PGA win to "elongate focus"? Remember him working with a rifle sharpshooter to "control heart rate"?

And that's just golf. Phil also studies philosophy, space, and literature. He explores astrology, the human body, and military history. He has an actual T. rex skull on his entryway table. Tiger? Tiger plays video games.

That kind of *Jeopardy!* mind that constantly yearns for something new, that kind of brain annoys the hell out of some people. Some caddies call him Carnac ("He's got all the answers"). Or FIGJAM (F*ck I'm Good, Just Ask Me).

Me, I love it, maybe because I'm the same way. People sometimes ask me: Why the hell would you quit the back page of *Sports Illustrated*, the greatest job in the world? And I say, "Because the back page of *Sports Illustrated* is a tiny corner of the world. It's a single Tic Tac in a single Tic Tac box in a 144-pack of Tic Tacs, which is part of a pallet of Tic Tacs, which are on the back shelf of a giant candy aisle of the massive food section of a colossal Super Costco and I wanted to see what else was in the store."

No matter where he is overseas, Tiger looks for a McDonald's and eats there. Phil travels the world and tries nearly everything.

I've petted lion cubs in Africa with him, gotten drunk out of the claret jug with him, had long off-the-record talks about his future and mine with him.

He's fabulous dinner company. For instance, at the yearly Masters champions dinner, "all the young guys try to get a chair at Phil's table," Jordan Spieth says. "Because you know Phil is going to be holding court." The year Australia's Adam Scott hosted, he served pavlova for dessert. When it arrived, Phil announced, with fanfare, "Pavlova was inspired by the Russian ballerina Anna Pavlova, when she was touring through Australia."

Everybody looked at him, dumbfounded. "I got $100 says that's not right," challenged Zach Johnson.

Phil took the bet, but since no phones are allowed at the dinner, nobody could Google it. They didn't have to. "See, my daughter was a dancer," Phil explained, pocketing the $100. "And she was doing a paper on Anna Pavlova, so I made 32 pavlovas for her class."

Well, what multimillionaire hasn't?

I've learned to never underestimate his research. The first season he and his brother-in-law joined the CBS fantasy football league, they won it with an 8–0 record, crushing no less than CBS's number-one NFL broadcast team, Tony Romo and Jim Nantz.

"You can talk to Phil about anything," says young superstar Collin Morikawa, "whether he knows the topic or not, he's going to say something."

OK, that's a bit of a complisult (compliment + insult = complisult). Phil usually *does* know what he's talking about. Once, I was trying to write a column about playing the new 15-inch hole, a concept that would make golf faster and more fun. I asked Phil about it, cold. Big mistake.

"Well, I did the math on it," he began. "The 15-inch hole is about four times bigger than the normal hole. That means a 12-footer is like a three-footer. So that means a 28-footer is like a seven-footer. I make about 50 percent of my seven-footers, so that means I'd make half of my 28-footers. My average length from the hole is about 30 feet. So I'd one-putt, on average, about half the holes I play. So I figure I'd shoot 14 under. That would be 58 on a par 72 course. On average."

I never wrote the column, but, Lord.

Tiger is famously distant with fans. He hates to sign or pose. At Pro-Ams, he's working on his own shots and doesn't give a warm pitcher of spit about yours. Phil, meanwhile, works every shot for any amateur who asks and many who don't. The world discovered that during *The Match* series. You could hear how much help Phil gave Tom Brady on every chip and putt. I mean, Phil won one of the things with Charles Barkley as his partner, so you tell me he's not a miracle worker.

"Phil is that annoying friend," Barkley said not long afterward. "You ask him a question...like, 'Hey, what's the weather like?' He says, 'You want the humidity, the barometric pressure, the high and low for the day?' No, man, I just want the damn weather...As great a guy as he is, when you ask him like,...'What do you think of this putt?' He goes, 'Well, it's down grain, it's into the grain, it's going to pull towards the valley.' Yo, man, just tell me where to hit the putt. I ain't got time to be analyzing down grain, up grain!"

Hey, Chuck, you're a 20 handicap. Maybe you should make time?

In whatever he does, Phil is *there*. He's into the moment, with both spikes. He even works hard on his pranks. Once, he and Ben Crane had a match against Tour pro Colt Knost and a writer who couldn't play dead in a horror movie. The writer was getting 24 strokes but Knost said it wasn't enough. He insisted the writer be able to play one tee up from the backs. Phil said sure. They teed off 1 and the writer got to tee off from about 30 yards closer. Off 2, the distance was about half that. By 4, the two tee boxes were only a few yards apart. That's when it hit Knost. He'd been had. "That son of a bitch," Knost thought. Turns out, Phil had called the pro shop and had the second tees moved closer to the tips from the second hole on in.

True, Tiger has had the far better career, has made more money, and will go down as the Best Golfer in History on a whole lot of lists. But he's also had the *Titanic* of sex scandals, a divorce, a stint in rehab, more surgeries than a MASH unit, a fractured relationship with his three half brothers, two arrests for driving while goofy on pills, and an unforced, no-skid-mark debilitating car wreck that nearly killed him. Phil, except for the Saudi screwup, meanwhile, has been largely scandal-free, is still married to the love of his life, has a great relationship with his siblings and his fans, has explored the world, and has the joy of being endlessly fascinated by it.

Whose life would you rather have?

Pagliacci

My favorite place in golf is across from David Feherty.

Drunk or sober, depressed or happy, lying in a hospital bed or in a Four Seasons suite, David Feherty is the most fun you can have without the use of psilocybins.

Feherty has been an opera singer, a golf star, an alcoholic, a clinically diagnosed depressive, a TV talk show host, a bipolar mess, a Masters tower announcer, a coke addict, a three-time bike-wreck survivor, a die-hard atheist, an opioid addict, surrogate father to Rory McIlroy, a $50,000/night after-dinner speaker, a writer, and a PTSD sufferer.

Yet, somehow, he remains the funniest man in golf. How can that be in the face of so much tragedy? "It's a self-defense," he says. "If I didn't have it, I'd be dead."

Growing up in Belfast, Northern Ireland, during the worst of The Troubles, he never knew when the next restaurant or office building would blow up behind him. Twice, the golf clubhouse where he worked exploded. "There'd be a call saying, 'Get everybody out of the building,'" Feherty recalls. "They'd get everybody out. Then word would go out and people in offices would come out with their office chairs, sit behind the yellow tape, and watch a building blow up. They'd go, 'Whoa, that was a f*cking good one!' They're scoring these things like the French ice-skating judge."

It gave him a case of PTSD that he's tried to cure ever since with booze, coke, "more pot than a Jamaican band," and whatever else might calm him down. Now he's getting medically induced ketamine infusions. "It's like being in Timothy Leary's electric chair," he says. "It's helped me. The first one, though, they didn't tell me you can't drive afterward. When I came to, I was buying a table and six chairs at an antique store."

He tried to replace the booze and the pills with biking, only to get hit by a truck, a lawn-equipment trailer, and a woman in a car. The truck almost killed him. "The lady in the car hit me and I just bounced right up, like 'Really, is that all you got?' But after that I lost my nerve. I couldn't get back on a bike." Every day he lives with a throbbing left shoulder, arm, and hand.

He is so honest about his miseries you almost ache for him. When his 29-year-old son, Shey, died of a drug overdose in 2017, three different presidents reached out to console him—Clinton, Bush 43, and Obama. "It doesn't get better," Feherty says of the grief. "It just gets farther away."

But Feherty is like a Whac-A-Mole. He just won't stay down. One night, not long after he'd announced he was trying to beat alcoholism, I saw him at a party.

So is this hard, with all the free booze around?

"Hell, this is the easy part," he said in that fabulous Irish lilt. "It's when I get back to the hotel room and that damn mini-bar is sitting there with the little bottles just taunting you in the little window and you've purposely told the front-desk clerk not to give you the little key and pretty soon you're throwing the thing around the room like a Kodiak bear trying to open a trash can."

The man is too funny for network TV. Once, early on in Tiger's career, Feherty was working the Masters from the tower at 15. Nobody had come close to reaching the second crosswalk with their drive, so the marshals were letting fans cross while Tiger teed it up. But Woods mashed it so far it came rolling down the fairway and toward the crossing. A woman in a long skirt and tennis shoes had to jump just to keep the ball from hitting her. "Oh well," Feherty told America. "The ladies have to lift their skirts for that one."

Feherty is part of golf history. He's been the canvas against which a lot of the world's best golf has been painted in the last six decades, from Nicklaus to Norman to Faldo to Phil to Tiger to Spieth. He's a walking, wisecracking Golfipedia.

Greatest player you ever saw?

"Tiger," he says. "Tiger Woods made me look like a moron more times than I care to count, and I don't need any help in that department. I'd give my opinion on what I thought was possible for a human being. I'd say, 'He's got to punch it out.' Then he'd hit some incredible miracle. He turned punch-outs into birdies. He'd pull off shots nobody else on earth would even attempt. And when he'd do it, oftentimes I'd be standing with the *next-*best player in the world, an Ernie Els or a David Duval, and I always thought they should cut to their faces at that moment, just to see the expression of 'What in the f*cking world just happened?' These guys would see these shots and go, 'Well, I don't have that, but I've got to try or I have no chance against this guy.' So they'd try impossible shots and not pull them off and get even farther behind. And that's how you win a US Open by 15 shots."

Phil Mickelson?

"When I'm following Phil I feel like a donkey looking at a new gate," Feherty says. "He does things I've never seen before. Sometimes, I'd look over at Bones (Phil's old caddy) with a bewildered look like, 'What in the world is he gonna do here?' and Bones would look back bewildered at me like, 'I have no earthly idea.'"

Greatest shot you ever saw?

"It wasn't on TV. It was on a Tuesday. We were playing Seve [Ballesteros] in a money game at Birkdale. He hit it into a bunker right of the green, right in front of the wall. The face of it was revetted and bone dry. The pin was also on the right and it was downhill all the way to the pin. I mean, f*cking impossible, no chance. Seve takes out a 4 iron. A 4 iron! And the three of us are like, 'What the hell's he gonna do with a 4 iron?' He opened it up and made this big 210-yard kind of swing. I mean, he hammered it into the face of the bunker, the ball hits the face, and, robbed of its f*cking will to live, just kind of flops onto the green and rolls to within four feet of the flag. I'm absolutely dumbfounded. And Seve turns to me, looks at my face and goes, 'What?'"

The Shark?

"Greg Norman was Tiger before Tiger was Tiger. He was like some kind of superhero. We'd wonder if he took his own train to the tournament. He had just an amazing sort of presence, this incredible confidence. Really, that confidence was one of the reasons he made such big mistakes. He was absolutely 1,000% committed to every shot, so if it was wrong, it was *really* wrong. That's what happened at that ['96] Masters [when Norman blew a six-shot lead]."

Feherty has known his own golf glories. The day he helped lead Ireland to victory at the Dunhill Cup at St. Andrews, he indulged himself in a bit of a celebration in the famed Jigger Inn just off the 17th and then decided, at 3:30 in the morning, everybody needed to play the 18th. He hit his drive, ran toward it, and fell straight into the Swilcan Burn, breaking his nose.

"But let the record show," he says. "I still made par."

For the love of Jesus, David, take care of yourself. Without you, golf is just oddly dressed people carrying odd-shaped sticks.

A Hook You Can Count On

At some point in a book like this, any golf writer must ask the obvious question: If you got all the living Tour players together in a big room...which one would kick the most ass?

Here are the bookmakers' favorites...

In this corner is Tony Finau. He's 6-4, 200 pounds, lean like a jaguar, strong like a bouncer, and trained to fight by his professional boxer dad.

So, Tony, is there anybody on Tour who could kick your ass?

He laughs. "No," Finau says, "because 99.9% of guys out here don't have near as much fighting experience as me. And not just in the ring. On the streets."

I'm looking at his face and he doesn't seem to be kidding.

In that corner is longtime Tour regular Pat Perez, a brawler who's been in more scrapes than a driver's ed teacher. For years, his headcover was a boxing glove. A former truck driver with a mullet and a chest the size of a starter's hut, Perez has such a bad temper, the PGA tried to get him into anger management classes. It didn't take.

In the near corner we have Ernie Els, the one they call the Big Easy. But Els is only easy until he's not. Once, coming from Tokyo to America on his private plane, he and his lone guest, touring journeyman Steve Marino, had already eaten and were having a few after-dinner pops when Els stood up, looked at Marino, and said, "Now, we fight."

Before Marino could say, "Wait. What?" Els headbutted him. Then they wrestled and clawed and gouged in the world's only flying cage match until one of the pilots came back and broke it up. "We had a lot to drink," Els admitted.

But here's the thing...I'll give you all *three* of those guys if you give me the little guy in the fourth corner, Esteban Toledo.

He's only about the size of a couch lamp and he's around 60 now but I guarantee you, Toledo could take any golfer alive with one hand and eat a ham sandwich with the other. Before he took up golf, he was a prizefighter in Mexico, with a 16–1 record and three KOs. He became a fine Tour player, but "I know I'm a better boxer than a golfer," he says.

You don't want any part of Toledo. In 2000, at a roadside Burger King in Tennessee, Toledo got out of his car to get a burger when two tall thugs came up and told him to give them his wallet.

"Why don't you come over and get it?" Toledo asked.

The first guy jumped him. Toledo knocked him down with a blurry left hook. That took about 10 seconds. Up came the other guy. Toledo eventually sent him to the asphalt with a straight right hand. That took about 40 seconds. Toledo was giving the guy's kidneys a free massage with his right boot when a third guy he hadn't seen jumped him from behind. You can guess how that worked out. All three of them ended up running for their lives.

"I don't hand over my wallet for nobody," Toledo says.

Can't blame him. He worked way too hard to put something in it. Toledo grew up with 11 siblings in a tiny dirt-floor adobe house in rural Mexicali, with no electricity, no running water, and no hope. Toledo didn't go to first grade until he was 10. He was too busy picking tomatoes and cotton and singing for pesos on buses. When his father died, 13-year-old Esteban was in charge of keeping food on the family table. So he started boxing as a pro. He was on his way to becoming a Mexican boxing star when appendicitis ended his career at age 20.

From there, he started shoveling dirt on the range at the nearby Mexicali Country Club. After a year, he was promoted to bartender. One day, on the TV behind the bar, he saw Tom Watson playing golf.

"Tom Watson was such a cool dude," Toledo remembers.

"I'd go outside with a club and try to swing like him...I knew right then I wanted to play on the PGA Tour and meet Mr. Tom Watson."

The problem was, he was terrible at golf. His brothers, caddies at Mexicali CC, wouldn't play with him because he couldn't break 100. So he played by himself on Mondays and got better. He learned a few English words. He met an American tourist named Jon Minnis. Pretty soon he was on a bus to San Jose to live with Minnis and his wife in their mansion. The first morning there, he walked outside to see a man in a tie standing next to a Mercedes limo. Esteban was afraid to get in.

"Where do we go?" Toledo asked the man.

"School," said the chauffeur.

It took Toledo until he was 32 to win his ticket to the PGA Tour, where they mistook him for a caddy, a gardener, anything but the man who would become one of the greatest Mexican-born players in history. It took until the 2002 Buick Open for the golf world to figure out how good he was. It was Saturday night and Toledo was tied with Tiger Woods for the lead. A reporter asked the 5-9, winless Toledo:

How do you feel about having to play against Tiger Woods?

Toledo stuck his chin out. "You need to ask him how he feels about playing against me."

Then a reporter asked Tiger:

You think you could beat Esteban in the boxing ring?

"Sure," Tiger said. "If I had a 2 iron."

Toledo never did win on the main PGA Tour, but last I checked he'd won four times on the senior Champions Tour and—even better—one of them was a one-shot win over a certain Mr. Tom Watson, whom he now calls a friend.

Which brings us back to our question:

So, Esteban, is there anybody in golf who could kick your ass?

"Oh, I don't like to fight anymore," Toledo says. "I'm capable of killing people if I have to, but, no. If somebody wants to fight me now, I just walk away."

Uh-oh. Better not get on Ernie's plane.

A Very Full Heart

Whenever somebody wins a Tour stop, an announcer with perfect hair will say, "This man has always had a very big heart."

OK, but has he had three?

If you could've seen Erik Compton as a kid, vacuuming up grounders at shortstop, you'd have thought his heart would never give out. But when he turned nine, doctors told him he had cardiomyopathy and he'd need a new heart—soon.

At 12, that new heart arrived. It belonged to another 12-year-old, a Tampa girl named Jannine, killed by a drunk driver. They rushed that part of Jannine to Miami's Jackson Hospital and transplanted it straight into Compton.

Jannine and Erik turned out to be a terrific combo. He played three years on the University of Georgia golf team and rose to be the number one amateur in the country. He feasted on golf's minor leagues, winning three times on the Canadian Tour and winning the Mexico Open.

But in 2007, at 28 years old, Jannine's heart gave out, too. Compton was practicing when he had a massive heart attack. Somehow, he got to his car and headed for the hospital, calling his parents as he went. "I'm dying," he told his mom, Eli. "I just wanted to say goodbye."

But killing Erik Compton is not that easy. He survived six more months until a new heart was found. It belonged to a high school volleyball star from Dayton, Ohio, named Isaac, killed in a hit-and-run when a truck struck his motorcycle.

Recovering in that hospital bed all those weeks, Compton would watch golf. Only the winner's face was never their face, it was his. "I'd see my friends doing great, so I just pictured my face over theirs, with my new healthy body, as they walked up 18. It gave me hope."

One thing about Compton, he hopes big. The average post-transplant life span is 9.1 years. Of those who get a second heart transplant, only 48% will live past a year. The idea that a man on his third heart would get up and go play professional golf at the highest level? Well, that would be in the National Journal of Crazy.

With Isaac's heart thumping inside of him, Erik Compton has gone on to play some of the best golf of his life. He got his Tour card in 2012 and then had the greatest week of his life—second place at the 2014 US Open. Just *think* of that: a man who has to take fifteen pills twice a day, whose resting heart rate is 96, who, according to the odds, shouldn't even be *alive*, nearly won our national championship. That preposterous achievement got him into the 2015 Masters where he made the cut, finishing fifty-first. What color jacket do you get for that?

One week—at the Memorial tournament in Ohio—he was having dinner with friends when the waitress said, "Hey, I read about you today. You're the golfer who had the heart transplant, right?"

Erik smiled and nodded.

"I know a little something about heart transplants," she said, "because my nephew, Isaac, was killed in a motorcycle crash. He donated his heart."

The table got eerily still. Erik looked up at her. "You're looking at the recipient," he said.

The waitress stood there stupefied. Then she came to Erik without a word. He rose and they hugged, wordlessly, for a long time. Feeling her nephew's heart beating against hers, she was overcome and ran into the kitchen in tears. The families are now friends.

"I'll never forget meeting Isaac's mother" says Eli. "I said, 'I'm Erik's mother. I know your son's heart went to my son.' It was overwhelming."

I think about that moment. One mother facing the other. One's utter loss the other's miraculous gain. One's grief, the other's joy. And yet, for Isaac's mom, knowing that her son's tragedy is helping another son do glorious things must bring a small dollop of joy into her pool of sorrow. The tapestry of every life is woven with other lives. We're all here together on this big blue ball, death brings life and life brings death and it starts all over again, an everlasting and bittersweet circle.

Isaac seemed to know that. In high school, he'd written a "mission statement" for his life. He wrote, *I will give service to others to help improve their lives.*

To me, Erik Compton should be the Comeback Player of the Year every year, for all of sport. I follow his scores wherever he goes. In 2021, I was covering the Colonial in Fort Worth, Texas, when Compton got hot and found himself in the top 10.

"I kept checking my heart rate," he said after that first round. "With all the self-induced emotions, it got up to 140 [bpm]." Heart transplant survivors can't slow their heartbeats down with deep, controlled breaths like the rest of us. Compton has to read putts with a Foo Fighters drum solo banging away in his chest.

No other Tour player "stresses their health every single day," as Compton says. No other Tour player has to fight through all the side effects of all those pills. No other Tour player has to deal with sudden, painful bouts of gout. One week, Compton was 6 under and right in the hunt when gout hit him so hard he had to withdraw. Can't recall that happening to Rory McIlroy.

Jannine's heart lasted 16 years. Isaac's is coming up on that same anniversary. Nobody, not even the specialists, know what will happen. There's no warranty on a heart, especially your third, but Erik's wife, Yessenia, is betting on her husband. "He's relentless," she says. "He's a little freight train. He just keeps pushing. He plays or practices every single day. He has more energy than anybody I know."

Compton doesn't lie in bed and scream at God. "He never feels sorry for himself," says his dad, Peter. "He could've decided to be the victim of the lousy hand he got dealt, but he just keeps at it. He's the most positive person you'll meet."

"Since I was 12 years old, every day has really been a gift," Compton says. "I think about it a lot. I'm out on the course sometimes and it hits me, how it's all a bonus. Life itself is a bonus."

CADDY

GOLF IS THE ONE place where a man who sleeps on satin will take advice from a man who sleeps on streets. Golf is like that. Golf is so hard it strips a guy down to his soul. The caddy, his only ally, gets a front-row seat to it. Which is why I spent a year caddying very badly for all kinds of famous golfers—from Donald Trump to John Daly to Bob Newhart— for my book Who's Your Caddy?

But the player who stuck in my brain the longest was Casey Martin, the golfer with a disability who took the PGA Tour all the way to the Supreme Court for the right to play a US Open out of a cart—and won. His right leg was riddled with Klippel-Trenaunay syndrome and yet he still could compete with the best in the world. Golf gods like Jack Nicklaus and Arnold Palmer railed against him riding in a cart, but riding in a cart was the last thing on earth Casey Martin wanted.

I caddied for him on the now-defunct Buy.com Tour in 2001 and was floored by just how much that leg plagued him. If he slept two hours in a row at night he was delighted. If somebody slapped it, he'd nearly black out in agony. It looked like a battered stick that had been chewed by beavers.

I carried the bag and he drove the cart, which he hated, trying to slip it through crowds and under ropes without getting decapitated. Then getting out and hoping not to accidentally step in a gopher hole and break that leg in half. It was all a kind of hell on wheels. But there was no other way. He could barely live with the pain, but he couldn't live without golf.

At any point, Martin could've chosen to forget Tour golf, amputate the leg below the knee, and guarantee himself a life of still being able to play buddy golf. But he wouldn't. If it broke above *the knee, he might never play again. "I know it will break someday," he told me back then. "I'm trying to get prepared for it."*

That day came 20 years later, in October of 2019. He was bringing the garbage cans in when he misjudged the height of the curb and his leg snapped in two. "I've never felt pain like that," he remembers. On the pain scale of 1 to 10? "A thousand," he says.

For two years, doctors tried to get it to heal. Finally, at 49, he checked into the Mayo Clinic for the dreaded above-knee amputation. He got hang-in-there encouragement texts that night from old Stanford teammate Tiger Woods, among a few hundred others. But he was still scared. When he came to, Martin felt a strange soup of grief and relief. Grief, because it was like losing a friend. After all, they'd done so much together. They'd not only won an NCAA championship at Stanford, they'd qualified for a year on Tour, played in two US Opens, and coached Oregon to the NCAA golf title. Relief, because it was like losing an enemy. That leg had plagued him for 40 years.

What are his one-legged golf dreams now? "Well, I talk all the time to people who play with a prosthesis, and they say I'll be amazed at what these things can do. Some of them can really play. So I hope to get back to that. Part of me thinks it'd be fun to play a few senior tournaments, get back out there and see what I can do."

Casey Martin is one of the bravest people I've ever known. Brave to play golf so well in such pain. Brave to take on the stodgy dandruffs who run golf for the right to torture himself.

"That's so cool you're going to keep competing," I said to him as he lay in his bed at the Mayo Clinic. "I'd love to be there, caddying for you, when you do."

"Absolutely not," he said.

———

SO HELP ME GOLF

Spieth to Me

You know the self-doubting, worrywart, inner-demon dialogue you have with yourself before you're about to hit a golf shot?

Jordan Spieth says all that stuff out loud.

He says it to his long-suffering caddy, Michael Greller. Spieth will be over a shot and launch into a TED Talk with Greller about an unfilled divot, or the lip of a bunker, or whether the wind will possibly change direction for the first time all day two seconds after impact. He is Rain Man. He will obsess with Greller on everything but how the flutter of a robin's wings will affect the flight of a punched 7 iron.

And what does Greller say in response?

"Yep." Except when he says, "Mmm-hmm." Occasionally, he will get wild and out with a "Sure."

The wonderful thing is, thanks to on-course microphones and golf announcers who've finally learned to SHUT UP—we get to *hear* a lot of these debates. They're glorious. I'd rather hear these two discuss the risks and rewards of a Spieth 6 iron over a creek than the entire Frost-Nixon interviews. Take this one from the Valero Texas Open, which we join midstream:

Spieth: It's about 90 from the bunker to the green though, right?
Greller: Yeah, but it's only 105 from RIGHT of the bunker.
Spieth: But it's only about 90 FROM the bunker right?
Greller: Yeah, but you're still trying to MISS it, right?
Spieth: Yeah, 100%.

They both laugh at the absurdity of it all.
"In college," Spieth says, "I'd just say all this stuff in my head.

Now I just tell it to Michael. I'm just blurting out whatever's in there...I'm sure he'd like to say, 'I don't care. Just get the ball in the hole before everybody else.' But he doesn't."

Greller, who is 16 years older than Spieth, was a sixth-grade teacher for years, so he's used to stream-of-consciousness rambling. He knows that sometimes young geniuses need to spew out all the junk before they get to that one spark of genius. And when it's nowhere near genius, Greller has that perfect teacher's tone—*Well, Jordan, should we maybe talk about what the consequences might be if it doesn't work?*

Exhibit A: At the 2021 Byron Nelson, there was a big chunk of crabgrass directly in front of the ball, and, farther ahead, a tree that was going to require a hellacious cut to get around, and, past that, water short and left of the green. You could almost hear the ball saying, "For chrissakes, *lay me up!*" Spieth, of course, wanted to go for it.

Spieth: If it goes left and it doesn't cut, it's fine, right?
Greller: Could come out short. I'm just saying.
Spieth: I think it [the clump] will affect it a little bit on the distance but not enough to leave it way short. Only thing it could do is affect the height.
Greller (ruefully): Hmmmm.

There's a long pause for deliberation and then...

Spieth: I'm fine with it.

That "I'm fine with it" is the equivalent of your mom yelling, "Not. Another. Word." It's when Greller knows it's time to back off and let this century's Arnold Palmer go to it. So Greller backed off. When your loop has made you, personally, about $4 million, you tend to let him do what he wants. Somehow Spieth carved an incredible cut around the tree, nearly hitting the flagstick 200-something yards away and making a birdie on his way to a 63.

Some of these Odd Couple episodes have gone into golf history. At the 2017 Masters, on the famous par 5 13th, with Spieth behind a tree above the fairway needing a colossal hook off pine straw to reach the green...

Spieth: What would Arnie do, Mike?
Greller: He'd hit it right below [the flag], 20 feet.
Spieth: All right, I'll do that.

And he did, to roars.

When you are carrying the bag of a human podcast, there are times to be quiet, times to be rah-rah, and times to be stern. "Sometimes he'll stop me when I'm going on too long," Spieth says. "Like after a bad shot I'll keep going on and on about it and he'll finally say, 'OK, that's enough now. We gotta let it go and move on to the next shot.'"

Because the Teacher and the Talent are so entertaining, the networks go to them now whenever possible, whether they're in the hunt or not. So when Spieth gets mad at his caddy—as every player does—the world knows it. At the 2019 Pebble Beach US Open, the boom mic was on Spieth when he snapped, "Two perfect shots, Michael. You got me in the water on one and over the green on the other." The snit was over by the next hole, but the internet hangs on to it to this day. "This is why I don't like Jordan Spieth," one person snarked under the video.

But what they don't know is how close these two are. "It's like he's my older brother," Spieth says. Brothers fight. Brothers get over it. Sometimes Spieth will airmail a shot over a green and say, "Five iron, Michael? Five iron? Really? You're fired." (He's kidding.)

What they don't know is that sometimes it feels like Greller is the one who's 16 years younger. "I can tell he's spent a lot of time around sixth graders because of the crap he eats," Spieth says. "He'll randomly just reach into his caddy bib and pull out half of an old Twix bar. Or he'll start working on some loose Goldfish. The other day, he pulls out a box of Nerds."

Doesn't matter. Spieth needs him.

"Michael just has a way to phrase things that help you see the other side. That's the sixth-grade teacher in him. He's great at explaining why it's a 7 iron instead of an 8. And that's when you're making your money, right? When you're slowing your guy down and getting him to take a longer look at something that ends up saving him?"

Right. It's all about getting to *I'm fine with it.* But what if Greller isn't fine with it?

"He has unlimited vetoes," Spieth says. "But he only takes a couple a year. He's right way more than 50% of the time, so if he sees me about to step into something that's going to be big trouble, I want him to feel free to pull me off it."

Once, on a dangerous hole at the Barclays, Spieth wanted to hit driver. Greller wanted him to play it safe.

Spieth: I like this because I think it gives me the best chance to make birdie.

Greller: Veto. I want you to hit 3 wood.

"I was like, 'Wow,'" Spieth remembers. "'OK, what choice do I have?'" He put the driver back and hit the 3 wood, then a 7 iron, and made birdie.

As they were walking off the green, Greller had a tiny smile on, which annoyed the bejesus out of the little brother. He turned to him and said, "If I'd have hit driver, I'd have made 2."

Two Dorks

The most popular win on Tour in 2021 wasn't Mickelson at the PGA or Rahm at the Open. It was Joel and Geno at the Puntacana in the Dominican Republic. It meant two of the funniest people on the circuit would be back for at least two more years.

Joel is Joel Dahmen, the player. He's certifiable. He's a one-man issue of *Psychology Today*.

He'll say "I suck so bad" at least five times on his way to a 64. He is allergic to practice. "I'm afraid if I practice, it'll make me think I can be really good," Dahmen reasons, "and then I won't live up to the expectations. That's no good."

Please email me if you follow that.

Geno is Geno Bonnalie, his giant bald-headed caddy. He's eight kinds of hilarious.

When his boss needs a short tee for a par 3, Geno will simply bite a long one in half. Cheaper than single-ply toilet paper, he drives a truck with 200,000 miles, no gas gauge, and no lights. He likes any Tour lodging as long as it's $39/night or less. "I feel like if I have a shower and a bed that's not gonna give me a disease, I'm fine," he explains. "I like to teeter on the disease line." He rents rooms straight out of a slasher movie and then shows the world just how disgusting it is on his popular Twitter feature "Caddy Cribs." One time he rented a house with no beds.

Joel and Geno have been best friends since junior high school in Washington. They both dreamed of being on the PGA Tour, but when Joel's talent lapped Geno's and Joel made it to the minor-league Korn Ferry Tour, Geno begged his wife to let him quit his well-paying job and go caddy for Joel.

Geno's Wife: How much money are you gonna make?
Geno: I might not make any.
Geno's Wife: OK.

Many times it's looked like a really dumb decision. Joel hit a wall that nearly ended both their golf careers. He couldn't get past the Canadian Tour. Then, in 2013, he failed again at Tour School and took a job holding down couch cushions in his living room. His girlfriend, Lona, was working two jobs to pay the bills. She finally told him either get back on the golf course or get a job.

He thought about driving for Uber or working the cart barn somewhere. He thought for a long time. Finally, he showered, dressed, and faced her.

Joel: Can I borrow $200?
Lona: What for?
Joel: A golf lesson.
Lona: OK.

That turned out to be a very good idea. Within months he was back punching 70 in the mouth nearly every day. He and

Lona got married, with Geno performing the ceremony using a $39 officiant's Universal Life Church license he got online. Geno likes things that are $39.

Soon, Joel and Geno were on the PGA Tour and Geno was tweeting to the world exactly what their very bizarre world is like. Like this moment from 2020:

Geno: 175 to the pin. It's a perfect 7 iron.
Joel: What about a smash 8?
Geno: The 7 goes 175. It's perfect.
Joel: I'm gonna hit 8.
Geno: I really think…
Joel: Stop talking.

(Joel hits the 8 iron 12 feet from the hole.)

Geno: You smashed that!
Joel: I had to. It was the wrong club.

Once, when it came out that worldwide superstar Rory McIlroy was going to change caddies, Geno sent him a letter, applying for the job.

He listed his qualifications, including the facts that:

a) He's "never, ever late."
b) His math skills are excellent. "What? You want 2% off 157 yards?" he wrote. "154. BAM. You want decimal points?"
c) His bunker raking is exquisite. "If they kept bunker-raking stats, I'd lead in every possible category."

Then he added:

"Please don't think I'm sneaking around behind Joel's back. Joel himself may be applying for the position."

It wasn't always funny. In 2011, Joel got testicular cancer, which was doubly scary since he lost his mother to cancer when he was in high school. Joel beat it, making him the only cancer survivor on Tour. You might have seen him wearing his giant sun hat with "~~Cancer~~" on the front.

Which brings us to that happy win in 2021, when Joel won the Puntacana, an official Tour event even if it doesn't sound like it. When the putt sank, Dahmen dropped his putter. Geno dropped the pin, which landed on the other player in the group. Then Geno stepped on the putter on the way to a massive hug they'd both dreamed about since they were kids.

It got better. At the awards ceremony, a gust of wind blew Joel's famous hat off. Geno, ever the faithful caddy, gave chase, jumped over a cliff, disappeared for a few seconds, and emerged with the hat, all the while not spilling a drop of his newly poured beer. It went viral.

"We are two golf dorks who grew up together," Dahmen says. "He's always been there for me. He's always believed in me. I always know Geno cares more about me than any golf shot I could ever hit."

Uh-oh. Better not show him the letter.

The Longest Long Shot

She's a skinny John Daly, a female Francis Ouimet, Walter Mitty in a ponytail. She's Sophia Popov and what she did at the 2020 British Open will go down in How the Hell Did She Do That history.

Here's how nuts her story is: when she did it, she was the 304th-ranked player in the world.

Now...the 304th-ranked chef in the world might be cooking at Applebee's. The 304th-ranked rapper in the world might not even have a single album. And the 304th-ranked female golfer in the world might not even get a ticket to *watch* a major, much less win one, right?

Ah, well, that's where Sophia pops in. She won it. Ms. 304 won the 2020 AIG Women's British Open. Yes, a woman who was caddying three weeks before, a woman who was pulling her own trolley in a tourney the week before, a woman who came into the thing as an 8,500-to-1 long shot, came to Troon in Scotland and made off with the biggest women's trophy in the world.

This is a woman who'd been ready to quit the game altogether. She'd fought Lyme disease for three years and was so tired and disgusted with the game that she started looking into master's programs at her alma mater, USC. She'd been a three-time All-American there, an achievement that felt like a lifetime ago.

She told her mom she'd had it and was thinking about changing careers. Her mom said, "Take two weeks off and then decide."

Mother knows best. Two weeks later, her daughter got back up and tried it again. "I just couldn't imagine letting the game get the better of me," she told friends.

And then a wonderful thing happened to Sophia Popov.

COVID.

"COVID gave me the best year of my life," she says.

OK, that's not a sentence you read much.

Here's what she means: When she missed her 2019 LPGA card by a single shot, it meant another year of having to scrape by on exemptions, weak fields, and Top Ramen. It meant when she wasn't playing the LPGA's bush leagues, she was doing nothing. Which is how she came to be caddying for her best friend on Tour, Holland's Anne van Dam, three weeks before the British. They finished 11th. But she learned something that week.

"Caddying, it hit me that you don't always have to go for everything," she says. "Anne wanted to go for every par 5 [in two] and take lots of chances. But I kept saying, 'No, why not lay up to wedge zone and make a birdie that way?'...And I started thinking, 'Why don't I tell *myself* to do that?'"

Then, thanks to COVID, players started canceling out of tournaments, like the Marathon Classic in Ohio, a week before the British. Popov got a last-minute entry and made the most of it, finishing ninth. After she signed her card, Anne came bounding up, all excited for her. What for? Sophia asked.

"The British Open," Anne explained. "Top ten make it in. You're in the British!"

Sophia was thrilled, but not for the golf. She was thrilled because making the British meant she was going to get to see her boyfriend of six years, German mini-tour pro Max Mehles. He'd lost his student visa three and a half months before and he'd been living with his parents.

"We just thought, 'This is going to be so fun. We get to be together!'" Popov remembers. She even thought it would be lovely (and save money) to have him caddy. But because her COVID test wasn't back early enough, she didn't arrive in Scotland until Tuesday night and only got a quick tour of Troon on Wednesday. Well, who needs practice when you're in love?

Then Thursday came and a funny thing happened. Putts started going into holes like mice running from cats. That's another thing COVID gave her a chance to do: learn to putt. She completely reworked her stroke. By Saturday night, she had a four-shot lead. Not that she knew about it. "I never looked at a leaderboard in four days," she says. "The leaderboard isn't going to change what I do, so I decided to just let Max handle it."

Scoreboards or not, Sophia was really nervous that Sunday. She bogeyed the first hole. The old Sophia would've thought, "Well, that was fun while it lasted." But the bogey just didn't seem to register with the new Sophia. What did register were the birdies on the next two holes.

And here's the other thing COVID gave her. Because there were no crowds, there weren't any roars for the four straight terrifying birdies Thai star Thidapa Suwannapura was making ahead of her. "So I didn't know anything about them," Popov recalls. "That helped."

When she and Max came to the par 4 18th, she didn't know she was ahead by three. "I figured it was one or two shots the way people were acting," she says.

Even a three-shot lead at a British Open isn't safe. (See: van de Velde, Jean.) Which is why, when her approach ended up in front of a yawning greenside bunker, her stomach was in her throat. She'd have to nip a perfect lob wedge off a tight lie, a shot that might not get over the bunker.

"I was thinking, 'Is the lead big enough for me to just putt *around* this thing?'" She turned to ask Max that very question. She didn't need to. He was walking toward her, holding the putter out. Why be the hero when you already *are* the hero?

She putted to the fringe and then lagged it to six inches. That's when it hit her: All that had been missing in her life was suddenly back. Missing so much time with the disease. Missing her card by one putt in 2019. Missing her boyfriend. It had all come home. She lowered her hat over her eyes and began to cry. She leaned into Max's big chest, gathered herself, came up smiling, and knocked it in for a 68 and an unthinkable win. "Three years ago, I wanted to quit," she told the press. "I'm SO glad I didn't."

She remains the lowest-ranked woman to ever win a major. And her 280-spot jump that next week is the largest in history.

There was one more little detail she hadn't thought about: the $675,000 she'd just made—six times what she'd won in her entire pro career.

"When that hit my account, it felt like, 'Is there something illegal going on?'" she remembers.

Yes, there is. You just stole the British Open.

Caddies Need Handles

A very brief list of my favorite all-time caddy names, for absolutely no reason...

MAD MAC—The Scottish caddy who wore no shirt, a long raincoat, and a pair of binoculars off a rope around his neck with no lenses. He'd use the binocs to read putts.

TWO SHOT LYNCH—So named because he was so grumpy, having him on your bag cost you two shots.

FLUFF—Got the name because he was unafraid of a joint in his off hours. "I don't smoke much," he told me once. "Just one on the front, one on the back, and one on the drive home."

CEMETERY—Famous Masters caddy who woke up in the morgue after surviving a knife in the throat.

FOOT—The late, great Pebble Beach caddy got the name via his promise that "You'll never have a bad lie with me, sir." Foot had a million stories, but always required me to buy him a "bit of the Robitussin" at the snack shack to keep his throat well-oiled for the telling.

ASBESTOS—Fire-proof.

LAST CALL—The former Tour player who drank himself into caddyhood. He once got an exemption into a tournament and beat his own guy, Jesper Parnevik, by two shots.

REPTILE—Never wore sunscreen. Remember the leathery lady who was Cameron Diaz's neighbor in *There's Something About Mary*? She looks pale next to Reptile.

TOP GUN—So named because he once gave his guy the wrong club, by two. The shot flew the green and buzzed the TV tower behind it.

BEAUTIFUL BILL BUSKY—His long, gorgeous hair never moved, even in the wind.

GOLF BALL—The caddy Ray Floyd fired six times, only to be hired back by Floyd's wife every time. When Golf Ball would get mad, his eyes would go as big as Pro Vs.

HERMAN—Lee Trevino's true and loyal Sancho Panza, a massive man of 400 pounds. Trevino loved Herman because he made putts easy to read. "Every putt," Trevino explained, "breaks toward Herman."

Mt. Humiliation

This is my 15th book, which sounds fun and glamorous until you factor in book tours.

A book tour is a device publishers invented to torture authors for taking advances. If you know somebody whose ego has gotten out of hand and needs to be cut down to the height of grasshopper socks, send them on a book tour.

For *Who's Your Caddy?* I went on a very long murderous book tour.

One snowy night, I found myself at the Mall of America in Minneapolis. I walked into the bookstore early and was flabbergasted at what I saw. There was a serpentine line of masking tape, starting at my signing table, through nonfiction, fiction, science, mysteries, children, self-help, past the cashiers, and out the front door.

There were a good 200 chairs in front of the podium. To the side were two long tables with mountains of Chips Ahoy cookies, painstakingly stacked into pyramids, each rising four feet high. Between the cookies were two giant orange coolers, one filled with lemonade and one with iced tea. Next to those were at least 1,000 napkins, 250 paper cups, and, for no apparent reason, 100 spoons.

I saw the young woman who seemed to be in charge, fussing with the chairs and directing two staffers to hurry out extra books for the signing. I went up to her and said, "Is Stephen King here tonight?"

She turned and said, "No, it's actually—" and then realized it was me and laughed a little. "Oh, hi, Mr. Reilly! Well, we expect a really big crowd tonight!"

One guy came.

One.

He was in shorts, a Vikings T-shirt, and flip-flops. He was maybe 35, a little pudgy, and had all the urgency about him of a guy who had nothing to do until a week from Thursday.

It was supposed to start at 7 p.m., but Miss Big Crowd wanted me to hold off. "Maybe they're parking," she said. "Mall of America is huge."

I hid near the travel section, hoping the floor would open up and swallow me down into the Gap below. It became 7:10. My audience was still sitting there, slouched in the very center card chair, first row, picking at his teeth. Now it was 7:15. I'm not a religious man, but I was praying that he'd leave. He didn't budge. I took the podium.

"Sir, do you want me to tell you about the book or just sign one for you?"

He beckoned me on with his hand, like a guy needing another card at a blackjack table.

Bring it on, Word Boy.

I sighed, took a big inhale, and went into it. I cut it down and finished in eight minutes and he was still sitting there, slouched.

He raised his hand to ask a question.

This guy was seriously trying to murder my soul.

"Sir, you don't need to raise your hand," I said with a sigh. "Go ahead."

He pointed over to the two long tables and said, "Can we eat them cookies?"

The Caddy Killer

For sheer James Bond thrills, peril, and escapes, my favorite player to watch was the late Seve Ballesteros, who played like a blindfolded man flying a helicopter. He'd hit insane hooks from the wrong hole. He'd make birdies from parking lots. He'd come flying out of forests with shots that never got higher than a poodle and yet somehow sizzled to a stop on the green.

Seve was constantly either livid or jubilant and nothing in between. One time, in the States, I had lunch with him when he was two shots off the lead. He looked like his house had just burned down.

Why so glum, Seve?

"This place, this Tour, iz not for me," he said. "These players, they are not my friends. They don't want me here. The food. I am no happy in this place."

So why don't you go back to Spain?

"Pah. Spain iz no good if you want to be the greatest."

Seve went through caddies like Taylor Swift through boyfriends. He was a card-carrying caddy killer. Once, after leaving a perfect 8 iron in a front bunker, he yelled at his caddy: "No, no, no, I do not blame you for this! I blame ME for hiring you!"

One time he airmailed an iron into the spinach behind the green. Naturally, it was time for the hit-and-whip. "You son of my bitch," he snapped. "I ask for yards. You give me meters!"

The caddy was his own brother.

Seve would get so ridiculously fired up during Ryder Cups he nearly self-ignited. I remember following him in a singles match against the American Tom Lehman. It was tense and the match was even. Seve was on the green and Lehman five yards off it. Lehman chipped up to within six inches for his par, but for some reason, Seve wasn't giving him the putt. Lehman looked over at him, twice, but Seve was stone-faced. No problem. Lehman simply tapped it in. Seve went nuts, yelling in Spanish at Lehman and hollering for a rules official. Seve told the official that Lehman played out of turn. He was right, but every other player on the planet would've given Lehman the putt and that would've been that. The official made Lehman mark his ball where it had been and wait. Seve putted up to within a foot and made his par. Lehman, so hot that steam was coming off his head, knocked his six-incher in for the second time. Later, I asked Seve, "Why'd you care so much?"

"Because," Seve growled, "I was going to use his mark as my line!"

Seve would do anything for an edge. When an opponent had a big tee shot to hit, Seve would suddenly decide to rearrange all the change in his pocket. Seve's friends would stand on a green and tell him in Spanish what the break was. One American player told me that during the Ryder Cup in Spain, European captain Seve was having certain greens mowed during the round and letting only his players know which ones they were.

But the best Seve story is his sudden-death playoff with Tony Johnstone of Zimbabwe. Seve had been up to all kinds of chicanery that day. He'd asked for four different rulings and gotten relief on all of them. Johnstone was about fed up to his collar button with him. So it was that they came to an uphill par 4. Johnstone hit his drive long and straight, the ball disappearing over the hill. Seve hit well, too, and Johnstone was off like he'd been shot out of a catapult. He was 100 feet ahead of Seve up the hill, almost in a jog.

When Seve crested the hill, he saw Johnstone next to a ball that was in the right rough and might have tree troubles. It was close to, but not quite bothered by, a French drain. Johnstone was talking to a rules official, trying to jerry-rig a phony stance that would afford a free drop away from the drain and also away from the tree trouble.

"No, no, no, Tony!" Seve yelled as he marched over to him.

"That's not a free drop! Nobody would take that stance for that shot!"

"Good," Johnstone said with a grin. "This is your ball."

The Green Mile

Some bags in golf are so hot they scald the caddy's shoulder. Mark Calcavecchia's was like that in 1995. The big, rumpled birdie machine had just won the BellSouth Classic and was on a roll. He took the check, hugged his caddy, Eric Larson, and said, "Buddy, I'll see you in two weeks."

But here it was, two weeks later, seven in the morning and no Larson. Eight a.m.: Nothing. Nine: Where the hell is E? "Finally at ten, I knew something was really wrong," Calcavecchia remembers. "E was never late."

Larson was late because Larson was in jail. He'd been arrested the day before in West Palm Beach, Florida, and charged with selling cocaine across state lines, a federal offense.

Nobody on Tour could fathom it. Larson wasn't a partier and he was never within a par 5 of trouble. He was as reliable as the sunrise. He'd been on Calc's bag since 1994 and they'd been inseparable ever since.

There was a story behind it. The year before, a friend got Larson to invest all the money he had—$250,000—in a health club he was building. The guy absconded with all of it. "That's when I think he turned to selling coke," Calc says.

What Larson had done was send small packages of coke from Florida to friends in the Midwest. He told the judge he'd never used the stuff, did it just to pay the bills. The federal judge didn't care. He hung 13 years on him.

Calc called him right before he went in. "When this nightmare is over," Calc said, "you've got a job waiting for you."

Why would a Tour star who'd won a British Open want a convicted drug dealer on the bag? Who knew what 13 years of striped sunshine could do to a man? Why? "Because Eric is the greatest guy," Calc says today. "He's so positive, so upbeat, so fun to be around. Everybody likes E. He's a great dude to hang with."

Calc did better than promise to hold Larson's job. He paid some of his attorney fees. He sent him money for the prison commissary. He visited him in all four of the jails Larson was transferred to, all over the country.

"Man, we'd sit there and talk and talk and four or five hours would fly by," Calc recalls. "But then, as I was saying goodbye to him, I'd think, 'Oh, man, I can't believe he's stuck in here for 11 more years.'"

Inside, Larson did everything he could to get outside. He wrote the judge who'd sentenced him and told him what he'd been doing—he had a garden, washed dishes for 12 cents an hour, and got his college degree. The judge wrote back, "I can't tell you how few letters I get from inmates. Thank you. Good luck."

Larson wound up serving 11 of the 13 years. When he walked out in late 2005, Calc, true to his word, was waiting with the caddy job. Phil Mickelson's caddy, Jim (Bones) Mackay, was waiting, too, with a slew of free clothes for him to wear. E was ready to start over.

Only one problem: under the terms of his probation, he wasn't allowed to leave Florida. No exceptions, his probation officer said. Little hard to caddy on Tour if you're stuck in one state.

Larson was poleaxed. His goal in prison was to caddy in a

Ryder Cup someday. Now he couldn't even leave the state? "I couldn't believe it," he says. "Dreaming of caddying again was what got me through. And now they weren't going to let me?"

But Larson never gives up in the middle of a round. He had one shot left to play. A week later, the probation officer got a very official-looking letter. "Eric Larson is still under my jurisdiction," federal judge Robert Holmes Bell wrote. "You will allow him to pursue his profession—caddying."

Remember the judge Larson had been writing about his garden? That was Judge Bell.

The first tournament back—the 2006 Honda Classic—Larson was on the range with Calc when a kind of millionaires' Welcome Wagon started wandering by. Phil Mickelson tapped him on the butt with a club and said, "E, it's good to have you back." Freddy stopped by, too. Bones. Everybody.

The good vibes were back, but the game was completely

different. Tiger Woods had changed everything. The purses were on steroids and it wasn't long before Larson got a chunk. When he and the now 48-year-old Calc won the 2007 PODS, Larson pocketed $75,000. That's 625,000 hours of dishwashing.

Since then, Larson's prison dreams have been coming real one after another. When Calc was almost 50 and ready to jump to the senior tour, young American star Anthony Kim asked Larson if he'd take his bag. But Larson was never going to turn his back on Calc, never, ever, never.

"If you don't take this bag," Calc said, "I'll never speak to you again."

Kim and Larson won two tournaments together and even got the first point Sunday for the USA in the winning 2008 Ryder Cup, the first US win in nine years. Kim beat Europe's Sergio Garcia so badly that when Kim went 5 Up on the 14th green, Kim didn't even know. He was striding to the 15th tee when Larson grabbed him and said, "You gotta go shake his hand. It's over."

"We still laugh about that," Larson says.

As I write this, Larson is on his 15th straight year on Tour without a miss. The strap on his shoulder now belongs to the solid Tour pro Harris English. They've already won twice together and been part of a historic American Ryder Cup win at Whistling Straits, Larson's second.

Larson blames nobody but himself for the years he lost. He doesn't talk about prison much. Still, sometimes between holes, young players will ask, "Dude, what was it like?"

Well, Larson looks at it like golf. When you've made a triple bogey, it's no good dwelling on it. You learn from it and move on. Next hole. "Prison sucks," Larson tells them. "But your friends get you through it."

MEMBER

YOU WOULD'VE LOVED MY mom, Betty. She was a stitch. One summer night she was taking me home from a baseball game. I was 11. We were at a stoplight, windows down. A car of high school boys pulled up next to us. The guy in the back was drinking a 40 ounce. He turned to her and said, "Go f*ck yourself, lady!" They all broke up laughing. When they stopped, she turned and said, "Not tonight. I have a headache."

She wasn't a bad golfer herself. One day, on page five of the Boulder Daily Camera *sports section, she and my dad and my brother all appeared in a photo together, each of them with a golf club and in a golf stance, commemorating the entire family's entry into the local Elks Club tournament. Secretly, though, I think she hated golf even more than I did.*

That was about the only time I can remember the light shining on my mom. The rest of her life was spent taking directions from men.

The youngest of seven kids, she was 22 and made to stay home and care for her ailing parents. Her father brought a guy named Jack home from a Knights of Columbus meeting and told her the two of them should now start dating. They started dating.

One night, Jack and his brother-in-law, Drell, got stinking drunk and Drell declared that Jack and Betty should get married, that night. My mother didn't want to get married that night. She wanted a real wedding, but they drove from Denver across the New Mexico line (no blood tests necessary), woke up the justice of the peace, and got married, with Drell along for the ride. No big wedding. No honeymoon. No nothing.

Her married life was lived in terror of my dad's drinking and even more terror at the idea of calling him on it. She was literally trapped, hiding in her room, waiting for him to pull the car out to go play golf so she could come out of the room and be with us kids. We begged her to leave him, but she was too Catholic.

One time, I was standing with her in the kitchen. My dad had just poured himself a tall 7&7, sat down with it in his La-Z-Boy, toasted himself, and said, "Well, here goes nothing."

To which my mom muttered to only me, "You can say that again."

My mom got a permanent dizziness the last 25 years of her life and no specialist ever figured out what was causing it. But I knew what it was. All that pent-up anger and frustration had nowhere to go. She had so many bottles of tranquilizers on her nightstand there was hardly room for the glass of water to take them.

Once a year, my dad would take us all out to dinner as a family, usually to Mr. Steak, where you could get a sirloin for $4.99. She thought it was thrilling. One night we'd ordered and were waiting for the food when she said happily, "Well, I wonder what the poor people are doing tonight?"

I looked around and said, "I think they're all at Mr. Steak, Mom."

That's one reason I wanted to join a country club, for my mom to be able to go somewhere nice, have Sunday brunch, be served like a fancy lady with cloth napkins and everything. But by the time I could afford to join one, my mom was too dizzy to come much.

I'd sit on the end of her bed and tell her what it was like playing golf with John Elway or how good the coq au vin was or what all the flowers were in the centerpiece and she'd clap her hands with glee, but that's as close as she ever got to the life she deserved. I was sure I knew who to blame for that.

———

The Red-Shoe Bandit

Now I have to tell you about Manny.

I've changed Manny's name here because I may kill him someday and I don't want to go to the chair for it.

Manny is the locker room attendant at the country club where I'm a member. Manny has the face of an altar boy and the heart of a Gambino. He's not much taller than a 5 wood, with perfectly parted hair, little black tie, and hands always folded neatly behind his back.

It's always... "Good to see you, Mr. Reilly" and "I hope you enjoy your round, Mr. Reilly" and "Anything I can do for you, Mr. Reilly?"

Yes, there is something you can do, Manny. You can swallow a grenade.

Take the other day. I'm at the airport. I have to check a bag, so I give my driver's license to a middle-aged United agent. Suddenly, she bursts out laughing and calls over a colleague. That woman looks at it and throws her head back howling.

"What?" I say.

Now the second gate agent has a couple of the bag guys over and they look at my license, then at me, then back again at the license and start rolling.

"What is it?" I say, louder.

She shows me the license. It says:

- Height: 6'0"
- Weight: 190
- Sex: NONE

Manny strikes again.

Apparently, I have this habit of not locking my locker while taking a shower and Manny works fast. What he can do to your wallet during a 10-minute shower would make a KGB agent jealous.

One time, I was pulled over by a cop and had to show him my license and registration. When he looked at the license, his eyes went big.

"Sir, this isn't you," he said. He had his right hand on my license and his left on his radio.

"What?" I asked.

He showed me without letting go of the license. Somehow, Manny had glued a picture of our head pro over my face. I guess it had been there for months and I'd never noticed. Who looks at their own driver's license photo?

"Oh my god," I told the officer. "I'm so sorry. It's this guy, Manny, he, uh, see, he likes to mess with me and...it's a...it's just a joke."

He didn't look convinced.

"Can I show you?"

He handed it to me. I used a fingernail to get the pro's face off my face. Thank god I was still under there.

The cop's granite face broke into a laugh. "That's f*cked up," he said. "Have a good day."

Essentially, I pay $1,500 a month for Manny to make my life a box of hell. I will open my locker to find the shelves full of women's intimacy products. I will open my locker to find it full of My Little Pony balloons. One time, I opened my locker to have 200 golf balls come cascading straight into my face. How much time does this kid have?

This all started about five years ago when I first met Manny. I looked at his innocent little face and thought, "Oh. This young guy seems nice."

Fool.

I had a pair of bright red golf shoes that I loved. Everybody else hated them. I finally saw what they meant and tossed them in the trash can near my locker.

When I came back to the club a week later, they were polished and back in my locker.

"Oh, Mr. Reilly," Manny said, arriving. "Somebody took your shoes and threw them out, so I put them back."

"Oh, no, man," I said. "I actually don't want them anymore, Manny. But thanks anyway." I picked them up and threw them back in the trash can.

The next week, they were shined and back in my locker.

"Manny!" I yelled across the room to him.

He showed up with his little tie and his little hands folded behind his back. "What can I do for you, Mr. Reilly?"

I held up the red shoes. "I told you I don't want these," I said. "You don't have to keep rescuing them. I don't want them. At all."

"Oh!" he said with perfect politeness. "I'm so sorry. I thought you were kidding, Mr. Reilly."

This time, I threw them in the dumpster in the parking lot. That was around Christmastime. I remember because of what happened at my Christmas party two weeks later. My buddy Brian Morris brought a present and put it on the counter. "I said no presents!" I said in mock protest.

"Ahh, it's small," Brian said.

I opened it. It was those goddamn red shoes. Brian admitted Manny was behind the whole thing.

I was starting to get a facial tic.

The next morning, I took the shoes, got in the car, drove three towns over, pulled off on an unknown street, saw a trash bin somebody had left on the curb, circled the block twice to look for Manny, threw it in park, got out, checked both ways, quickly threw the shoes in, and peeled off.

As I drove away, I checked my rearview mirror one last time. Seeing nothing, a maniac's grin overtook my face and I cackled, "Goddamn Manny thinks he's gonna get in MY head?"

Traditions Like No Others

In Denver, a man named George Sarkos begins every round by hitting a tee shot with his best friend Brett's name on it. Brett died of brain cancer years ago, but George still misses him every day, so he leaves that ball out there just to let him know.

At Bethpage Black in New York, entire foursomes sleep in the parking lot overnight to get one of the first tee times of the day, thus providing the answer to the question: What would you shoot if you played one of the most treacherous courses in the world after sleeping in the back of a Toyota Camry? (A: The approximate weight of a high school tuba player.)

In San Francisco, when you get to the 17th tee box at Lincoln Park, you turn 90 degrees away from the hole, tee up an old ball, and try to split the uprights formed by the Golden Gate Bridge. It makes no sense, since the bridge is a good 5,000 yards away, but when has golf ever made sense?

I love that kind of stuff. I love all the wonderful little traditions golf has everywhere you look.

Years later, you'll never remember what you shot at Old

Memorial in Tampa that day. But you'll remember the birdie you made at the 10th and how they made you sign the ball and leave it at the base of the statue of the two beloved members they lost on 9/11. It's a tradition.

I love that the caddy of the winning player on Tour in any week has to buy his caddy buddies a chicken dinner somewhere down the road, beers included. (Thus, the supposed origin of "Winner, winner, chicken dinner.")

I love the club in Dallas, Oregon, where men must don the pink batting helmet if they don't hit their first drive past the women's tees.

Or the way you leave a bottle of your favorite bourbon on the first tee at Peyton Manning's Sweetens Cove in Tennessee, then take a mandatory shot from one of the bottles that are already there.

I love Ballyneal in Holyoke, Colorado, where the losing team has to carry the winning team's bags up the hill to the clubhouse, for all the members to see.

I love taking off my hat on 18 to shake hands. I love your opponent searching for your ball even if finding it means he loses the match. I love that nobody cheats their friends, even when nobody would ever know. OK, almost nobody.

Have you ever stood on the first tee at Riviera Country Club in LA? You stand on this tiny little bath mat of a tee box and the majestic hilltop clubhouse and its members are practically in your backswing and Mark Wahlberg is just finishing his 18-hole sprint over here and Larry David is singing something unrecognizable over there and the earth drops 100 feet right in front of you. That's when a man comes out of the little hut there with a clipboard and bellows: "Riviera would like to welcome—from

Des Moines, Iowa—Morty Schnerdlap!" As if you weren't nervous enough.

OK, there are traditions you might not like. At Preston Trail in Dallas, no women are allowed on premises. *Ladies, wait!* Before you picket, you might want to hear about what you're missing. Nobody has to wear a shirt at Preston Trail. For that matter, nobody has to wear pants. Nobody is even required to wear underwear. They say Mickey Mantle once played 18 holes buck naked. You can even eat your lunch *sans* clothes, but for god's sake, wrap a towel around you before you dig into your bowl of chili. So, women of America, you SURE you want in?

If so, look no further than the La Jenny golf course near Bordeaux in France, where everybody plays nude. The lawn maintenance is said to be exceptional, however.

My favorite tradition in golf, though, is the one at Royal Dornoch, a place so far north in Scotland even William Wallace never went there. I did, though, for a week of golf school. After tapping in on 18 at the end of the first day, I thanked my weather-beaten, ruddy-faced, sawed-off caddy Sandy and said, "I'll see you in the morning."

He just stared at me.

"What?" I said.

"Will ya nay partake of the tradition, sir?" Sandy said.

"Tradition?"

"Aye. Ye buy your caddy a wee dram of scotch, sir."

"In the bar?"

"Aye."

"Well...sure."

So we went up to the bar and before Sandy had even taken any of his three coats off, the bartender set a dram of Macallan scotch in front of him. Apparently, Sandy had partaken of the tradition before. I got one, too, my first Macallan. The warmth in my chest thanked me. Sandy had said about six words all day and I suddenly was in the mood for some human interaction.

"Sandy, have you drank Macallan your whole life?" I asked.

He took a sip, put his glass back down, wiped his mouth, and said, "Not yet."

Club Pro Guy

Is he a real person or a fictional character? Does he really hide his face because he owes money to Mexican drug cartels or does he just not want his boss to know he's a fake and hilarious Twitter sensation? Is he really a Mexican mini-tour legend? *Is there* a Mexican mini tour?

Whatever he is, Club Pro Guy, the head pro at a Kansas City country club he won't name, is a very tough get. After years of trying, I was finally able to wrangle him to answer a few questions, as long as I deleted my entire hard drive afterward.

Q: *CPG, thank you for this. You've had so much success in your career. Have there been any low points?*

CPG: Anyone who begins his Tour career by missing 44 straight cuts is going to have some low points. But if I had to name just one, it was probably the '95 Tecate Cup matches against Guatemala. I was a playing captain. Not only did I go 0–5–0 in my matches but we lost 23–5. To make matters worse, I found out my wife, Brandi, had sex with most of the players on our team and five of the Guatemalans.

Q: *Oh man. I'm sorry. Any other low points?*

CPG: Well, late in my career, I signed a contract with US Kids Golf Corp. I didn't notice, in the fine print, I was obligated to play *their* equipment. I had to use a 35" driver for the better part of two years. It ruined my game.

Q: *Your documentary,* The Streak: 8 Straight Pars to Glory, *will be out soon. Did the reality of what you were accomplishing hit you at the time?*

CPG: I don't think people will ever fully appreciate the weight I carried during that streak. It ended, unfortunately, on the second leg of El Chapo's Taint. In my defense, the second hole of the Taint is probably the tightest hole we played on Tour.

Q: *Your career had a lot of controversy. Were you ever DQ'd?*

CPG: I was DQ'd at the '92 Todos Santos Open for having a double-sided chipper in the bag. It hurt because I was probably going to make the cut. I had no idea those were illegal.

Q: *You're a famous money game player. What's the best way to get somebody to give you a putt?*

CPG: I love digging in my pocket for a mark for an inordinate, almost painful amount of time. But I've found the best way is to look them straight in the eye and say, "Do you need to see this?"

Q: *Smart. How big is your circle of love?*

CPG: The size of a standard hot tub.

Q: *Part of your club pro job is teaching. Got any swing tips for my readers?*

CPG: I don't do swing "tips." I deal in swing "thoughts." Here are a few of my favorites:

Left elbow points towards Mama's house.
Scratch that itch.

Count to three, then let it go. STOP! Now go. WAIT!
The club is a snake.
Check the watch. Hold it. Now it's go time.
Don't go right, don't go right, don't go right...F*CK!
Lietzke '81.
Right heel, you been a bad boy.
Belt buckle don't lie. Then let it fly.
Turn. Wait, what? Hammer time.

Q: *Wow. That's a bunch. Hey, why did you give up on the "stack and tilt"?*

CPG: I did it for three years and then accidentally discovered I was tilting, then stacking.

Q: *What putting stroke are you using now?*

CPG: It's a hybrid between Billy Mayfair in his prime and getting tasered.

Q: *Any golf rules you think are unfair?*

CPG: If I say "put me down for a 5" when I actually had a 6 and my playing opponent doesn't object, then I should get a 5. Half of golf is about paying attention.

Q: *Which of your students have you found the most fulfilling to work with?*

CPG: Probably Shelby Clayman. She's 42 years old with implants and a major sauvignon blanc problem. She lives just off the fourth green and her husband Barry travels to Omaha a ton for work.

Q: *What touches do you give your members that most clubs don't?*

CPG: We stack our range balls in pyramids, which is cool. We also rotate our driving range mats 90 degrees every few months to distribute wear and tear.

Q: *I'd love to play your course but it's private. Any way around that?*

CPG: The best way is to buy a Groupon because they get the best tee times. Between Groupons and wall-to-wall corporate outings, our members have very little access to the golf course.

Q: *It took so long for me to get an interview with you. Maybe you've had trouble in the past with golf writers?*

CPG: It was prickly at times because I recognized early on that the media has an agenda. If I shot 88, they would just simply report the score and give no mention to how many edges I burned or how many shots I left out there.

Q: *I guess that's why, unlike so many stars, you wrote your own autobiography. What's it called?*

CPG: *Club Pro Guy's Other Black Book.* It's a collection of my tips and wisdom on almost four decades in the game.

Q: *Any examples?*

CPG: Well, there's a story in there about the time I actually met Jay Don Blake. One of the defining moments of my life.

Q: *I'll bet. Last one—if you'd never been introduced to golf, what would you be doing in life?*

CPG: My sister owns a Curves for Women franchise in Wichita so I imagine I'd be involved in that in some capacity.

The Optometrist

Like a lot of stuff at a country club, the process to join is full of fiery hoops you have to somersault through, held by stuffed suits who would prefer you'd just give up. The final hoop is the one where you sit down in front of the board of directors.

It's scary unless you've done it before, which I had. But the little bespectacled optometrist sitting next to me hadn't and he looked petrified. We were going through together—both of us complete strangers to each other—and he was as nervous as Stormy Daniels at a First Communion.

"What do you think they'll ask us?" he said as we waited.

"Aw, it'll be easy," I said. "Probably just about how much we'll play, are the kids going to be at the pool a lot, stuff like that."

The door opened and a bony mortician-looking guy motioned us in. The nine of them were a foot above us, sitting at a big desk. We sat in two little chairs. Welcome to the Warren Commission.

An old fossil started by saying, "So, Rick, do you think Tiger will pass Nicklaus?"

Ahhh, this was going to be a lay-up.

"I don't think so," I said, sitting back in my chair. "And here's why…" Then I proceeded to answer that question and 20 more. They wanted to know about Hogan, Mickelson, and everybody in between. I gave them all they could eat.

Finally, after about a half hour of my answering their questions, Mr. Bony escorted us back out and told us to wait while they voted. That's when it hit me. The optometrist hadn't said a single word. They hadn't asked the poor guy a single question. His face was ash white.

"Oh my gosh," he moaned. "Nobody told me we had to know so much about golf!"

I got in, but he got blackballed.

I'm kidding…He got in.

Bar Bets

I know too much about golf. It's a little sad. My buddy Skybox will be trying to decide which club to hit and I'll say, "Did you know Walter Hagen won most of his 11 majors with 20 irons and four woods in his bag? There was no club limit back then."

Skybox will roll his eyes. "Fascinating."

Pebble Beach will be on TV and I'll say to my son Kellen, "Did you know the two men who designed Pebble Beach had never designed a golf course before and never did one afterward?"

Kellen will pop a Cheeto in his mouth and mutter, "Riveting."

Someone will tell me that gonzo journalist Hunter Thompson is their favorite writer and I'll say, "Did you know he had a golf course at his ranch in Aspen where the only way you were allowed to advance the ball is with a shotgun?"

That tends to kill the conversation fast.

I'm telling you, get to know me. You could win a lot of bets.

Throw these out at the bar tomorrow night, and if anyone calls you a liar, watch the cash roll in.

You simply say, "Did you know..."

- Justin Rose missed his first 21 cuts in a row?
- Phil Mickelson does everything else right-handed?
- Tiger Woods can hold his breath for six minutes? He can. It's handy for spearfishing off his yacht, *Privacy*.
- The most dominant high school golf coach in America is a nun? Sister Lynn Winsor's Xavier Prep girls teams in Phoenix have won 36 straight state championships.
- Irish star Rory McIlroy once hit a drive at the Masters that hit his own father?
- TV great Jackie Gleason carried 12 woods, all of them with mink headcovers?
- Baltusrol, the New Jersey club that's hosted nine majors, is named after a murdered man? The dead man was Baltus

Roll, who, in 1831, refused to reveal the location of his fortune to two assailants who beat him to death trying to get it out of him.

- Whenever Ernie Els makes a birdie, he throws out the ball? He believes no golf ball has more than one birdie in it.

- Only one person has been allowed to take his Masters green jacket home for good? That was 1970 champ Billy Casper, who got permission to be buried in it.

- Crail in Scotland, designed by Tom Morris, has two fairways that crisscross each other? I know because my son Jake got hit right in the no-man's-land.

- A sultan in Malaysia once killed his caddy? He was playing in 1987 when he whiffed a 3 iron. His caddy laughed at him. The sultan buried the 3 iron in the caddy's skull.

- At the 1945 LA Open, Sam Snead won playing one ball the entire 72 holes? He stuck with it, even as the cover was coming off. There was a national rubber shortage.

- Bubba Watson, who draws giant crowds, has a fear of them? When he hit his incredible left-handed hook wedge from the trees off 10 to win the 2012 Masters, the first thing he said to his caddy upon escaping the throngs of people was not about the unforgettable shot or his imminent life-changing victory. What he said was, wriggling like he had spiders in his shirt, "Those people were touching me!"

- Tiger Woods is allergic to grass?

- Arnold Palmer, who signed more autographs than any person in history, had a pen with disappearing ink for people who were being rude to him? The autograph would vanish within 20 minutes.

- Until he won the 2021 British Masters, Richard Bland hadn't won a single tournament in all his 23 years on the European Tour? Yep. He was 0 for 477 until that day.
- According to the USGA handicapping website, GHIN.com, President Joe Biden is a 6.7 handicap at Fieldstone Golf Club in Delaware? And Caitlyn Jenner is an 8.0 from the women's tees at Sherwood in California? And Larry the Cable Guy is a 9.0 at Firethorn in Nebraska? And Phil Mickelson is a +6.6 at Whisper Rock in Scottsdale, Arizona?
- Jack Nicklaus is color-blind?

A Movable Feast

Among the thousands of reasons golf is better than any other sport has nothing to do with the sport at all.

It's the food.

In the middle of a volleyball match, you cannot stop and be handed Merion's famous bacon, peanut butter, and jelly sandwich, which is so dang tasty you wish Elvis were alive just so you could watch him drool on his white pantsuit.

In the middle of a pickup basketball game, you cannot stop and slurp the corn sausage chowder at Blackwolf Run that is so delectable it would make a Boston chef hurl a can of beans.

Let me ask you, in the middle of your last triathlon, did you stop on the porch at Sunningdale in England and savor the homemade chocolate caramel shortbread set before you?

But above all, only in golf can you eat the Burgerdog.

The Burgerdog is proof that God loves us. That's literally true. At the Olympic Club in San Francisco, where the Burgerdog was invented, there hangs a certificate from the archdiocese of San Francisco decreeing that "by special dispensation from the Archbishop, Catholics may eat a Burgerdog on Fridays."

The Burgerdog is an invention of simple genius—a cheeseburger served in a hot dog bun. It's not only wildly delicious, but it can be eaten with one hand, meaning you can play on, if you can make par with burger juice dripping down your chin. It was invented one day by a between-gigs trumpet player named Bill Parrish, who pulled up his tiny trailer outside Olympic one day in 1950 and started grilling up burgers and dogs so good that members would send caddies over the fence to get them. Some say that one day Bill ran out of hamburger buns. Others say Bill wanted more room on his grill so he started shaping them longer and skinnier. Either way, golf grub history was made.

For some, the food is the main reason to play golf at all. I have a very tall friend, Cliff, whom I play with one morning a week at a course that's famous for its lovely lunches. The worse he plays, the sooner he begins talking about lunch.

Cliff: Whaddya think?
Me: What do I think what?
Cliff: The gazpacho? Or the chicken tortilla soup? You know, for starters?
Me: I don't know, Cliff. We're only on the third hole.

Forgetting fried eggs and chili dips, food has figured in much of golf history. When Arkansas native John Daly won the 1995 Open Championship at St. Andrews, he credited the homemade chocolate chocolate-chip muffins a lady was selling each day on the course. "They were the good kind, too," Daly said, clutching the claret jug. "Them Otis Spunkmeyer kind you get at the Sinclair stations back home." You should've seen the faces of the Royal & Ancient dandruffs drop.

Our golf memories are flavored by the food we ate playing it. "Back in the '70s I would tag along with my grandfather and my uncle as they played at Shorecliffs in San Clemente," John Kevari recalls. "I was a nine-year-old kid and my grandpa would bring peanut butter and jelly sandwiches. I'll never forget that. Sitting in a golf cart between the 9th and 10th hole in the sunshine and I didn't have a care in the world. Oh, how I wish we could have one more lunch together."

After years of dedicated munching, I've compiled the Official and Irrevocable 10 Best Things You Can Eat in Golf.

1. The Burgerdog, Olympic Club, San Francisco.
2. The chocolate-mint milkshakes, Castle Pines, Colorado.
3. The lobster lunch, the National, New York.
4. The Loco Moco, Plantation Course, Hawaii, an impossible orgy of juicy burger, fried egg, blissful gravy, and sticky rice. I know, I know, but you have to try it.
5. The delectable egg sandwich at Seven Canyons, Sedona, Arizona. When you play Seven Canyons, two things will make your mouth drop—the sky-piercing red rocks all around you and this egg sandwich.
6. The homemade warm chocolate chip cookies at the end of your round at Cascata, near Las Vegas, the ones that make you think of your sweet mother and then hang your head at the vile shames you committed the night before.

7. The shrimp grits at Congaree, South Carolina. Lordy, lordy.

8. The hot baked potato, split open and filled with beans, bacon, and cheese, served from the Potato Truck, which parks itself on the front nine at every Open Championship. (Some sportswriters will tell you that their curry one is better, but these sportswriters are godless Communists.)

9. That ridiculous chowder at Blackwolf Run, Wisconsin.

10. The free hot chocolate and Baileys they bring you on a numb-fingered day on the back nine at Silver Lake in Scottsdale, Arizona. Why do they do this when you didn't even ask? Because they are saints who walk the earth and should be given many kick-in birdies in their lives.

Puddles

One day, two actors—Jack Nicholson and Joe Pesci—were playing a rather tricky 175-yard uphill par 3 at a star-packed Los Angeles country club.

Neither was particularly good at the game, but neither was particularly awful, either. They both liked to play fast, smoke cigars, and enjoy the fruit of the mulligan tree, so they often played together.

Nicholson was on the tee, about to hit a 5 wood, when he noticed a small fluffy white poodle wander across the fairway. It seemed to have escaped from the confines of the big house that hung over the green on the right side.

He stopped and watched, seeing as how it's not often you see a fluffy lap dog cavorting along a fairway. Suddenly, a huge red-tailed hawk came swooping down from the sky, snatched the

poodle up with his big talons, and made off with it, over the trees and out of sight.

Nicholson and Pesci couldn't believe what they'd just seen. You hear about these things happening on a golf course, but it's rarely witnessed. And yet there it was.

After staring at each other awhile in awe, they shrugged and hit their shots. They were halfway up the hill to the green when a fifty-something woman in bathrobe and curlers came to the balcony of the big house and hollered, "Puddles!...Puh-dulls!... Come home for breakfast!"

That's when Pesci took the cigar out of his mouth and yelled, "Lady, Puddles ain't comin' home for breakfast, lunch, nor dinner, neither!"

INTERMISSION

Stuff I Hate

And now, a brief interlude, to tell you a few things I *hate* about golf.

One: Impact idiots.

I guess I've been to 500 golf tournaments and I'm still waiting for a fan to yell something funny after impact. Thousands try and thousands fail. I remember when it started—the 1979 US Open in Toledo, won by Hale Irwin. There was this moment when Irwin hit his drive and a huge voice hollered into the silence, "You da man!"

That got old after about the third or fourth one and yet it continued for *20 years*. Then we entered the Era of Idiots. Fans started yelling "Get in the hole!" constantly, even on par 5s. "Baba Booey!" "Mashed potatoes!" "Boom goes the dynamite!" (OK, the first time, that one was a little funny.)

I'm not saying these people don't have the right to do it. I'm saying I should also have the right to strap these people to a table and have Tabasco dropped into their eyes. "I think they should allow the players to take 10,000-volt tasers," Ian Poulter once tweeted, "and taser every muppet who shouts out something stupid."

Look, we know, Clever Guy. Before you left for the course this morning, you told your bros to listen for it and they'd know you were there. Can't you just bring them a ticket stub? I mean, do we come to your job while you're working and holler, "Super-size it!"?

Two: Holes with names.

Golf club owners of the world, listen up. Nobody looks at the stupid little names you dream up for each of your holes. Nobody cares that the third is called Old Tom Morris and the 18th is called Home Again. You're wasting space on your scorecards reminding us that 7 is Peach Blossom and 16 is Lotus Flower. These names are the equivalent of "Important Changes to Our Privacy Policy" we see and don't read 100 times a month on our iPhones. You could name all 18 holes after strippers and we wouldn't know. Nobody is going to say, "Hey, I birdied Mystique!"

Three: Golf-cart music.

I love music. I listen to my music nearly everywhere. But notice I didn't say *you* listen to my music. You don't have to. I wear head-phones. I figure we have a deal. I won't subject you to my Miles Davis and you don't subject me to your Toby Keith. Besides, golf is its own music: the perfect thump of a wedge, the satisfying rattle of a putt dropping. But I can't hear any of that because you're bumping Metallica at a level that makes dogs hide. Can't we have one place where we can actually hear the birds singing, the branches rustling, the brook lapping? One time, I was playing and I heard a commotion in the woods. Suddenly, two bucks came tumbling down the hill, their horns locked in battle. I don't want to miss that next time because you're thumping Ol' Dirty Bastard.

Four: Quoting **Caddyshack**.

It's been 40 years. We know, we know, we know. "Noonan." "Big hitter, the Lama." "That's a peach, hon." All that. Those stopped being funny just after *Thriller* came out.

What you need is some new stuff.

Luckily, I'm here to help. Use these next time...

...somebody poses too long over a good tee shot: "Pick up your flowers, Tiffany, and get off the ice."

...somebody hits a massive drive: "I feel sticky."

...somebody hits a drive way out of bounds: "Recalculating."

...your friend is wearing a really bad shirt:

You: "You want us to get the guy?"

Him: "Who?"

You: "The guy who made you wear that shirt."

...a bad player finally makes a par: "Congratulations. Go paint the town beige."

...your partner makes a huge putt: "Film at 11."

...your friend hits it out of bounds off the tee: "That's a Princess Diana. Shouldn't have taken a driver."

...you're with a slow player: "Hold up. Betty White wants to play through."

...somebody has really old stuff: "Hey, Herbert Hoover called. He wants his clubs back."

...somebody hits a really bad tee shot: "That's a Rush Limbaugh: fat, high, and way right."

... your opponent wants you to give him his four-footer: "Still a little left there, Lorena."

... the line on a putt is just outside the hole: "That's a Lance Armstrong. One ball out."

... somebody slices everything:

You: You should be on Tinder.

Him: Why?

You: Because you swipe right a LOT.

... you don't see any break in your partner's putt: "This is a Tom Cruise. It doesn't look straight. It can't be straight. But it IS straight."

... somebody misses every fairway: "You drive worse than Tiger."

... you hit a putt that's going to be short: "Break a tackle!"

... a shot takes off fine but then goes bad: "That's a Meg Ryan. It was pretty for a while."

... your partner is facing a really steep putt: "Careful. This thing is faster than Chris Christie on a waterslide."

... your guest at your club shoots 107:

Him: What do I owe you?

You: A damn apology.

Five: Poor Tiger.

I hear this all the time. "Poor Tiger." As in ... "Oh, look what poor Tiger's been through."

Been through? Did he get hit by a bus (Ben Hogan), get cancer (Paul Azinger), or overcome a genetic defect (Casey Martin)? Nearly everything that Tiger Woods has "been through" have been unforced errors.

Remind me, did somebody force him to take all those pills

and get busted for it while driving (twice)? Did somebody hold a Glock and make him fly over a median, cross through two oncoming traffic lanes, and smash into a tree, totaling the car and nearly himself? There were no skid marks, meaning he never hit the brakes. What if your daughter had been in one of those lanes?

When he got himself into one of the worst sex scandals in modern American history, was it the fault of the Swedish bikini model he was married to?

When he was "training" with the US Navy Seals and hurt his knee on parachute jumps, was he in Afghanistan?

Look, Tiger Woods is the greatest single golfer I've ever seen. Jack Nicklaus had the better career, but nobody in history had the skills of Tiger Woods. But he's terrible with fans, a rotten tipper, and has something eating at him that he doesn't seem to want to deal with. Golf skills? Hell yes. Life skills? Not many.

Six: Lifetime exemptions.

What if the Academy Awards started allowing old actresses a chance to win Best Actress when they hadn't been in a movie in years? Insane, right? So why in the world does the Masters, the Open Championship, and the PGA Championship do that exact same thing?

For some reason, those three majors let old, dusty champions take up precious spots without doing a thing to earn them, spots that could go to a player with an actual snowball's chance.

At the 2021 Masters, six players who had no hope were given spots—Larry Mize ('87), Sandy Lyle ('88), Ian Woosnam ('91), Fred Couples ('92), José María Olazábal ('94), and Vijay Singh ('00). All fine champions once, but do you put Jimmy Carter on the next presidential ballot because he won it once? And what did those guys do that year with their spot? They went +19, +12, +9, +13, +8, and +15, respectively.

The Open Championship lets past champions play until their 60th birthday if they want, which is what made the 2018 championship at Carnoustie feel like an assisted-living outing. The 2021 PGA was a Who's Not Who of golf.

They should all do it the way the US Open does it, which is: Look, you won. Good for you. Here's 10 years' free entry. If you can't win it again in the extra decade we give you, we'll see you at the Tuesday dinner.

OK, I feel better.

DEFENDER

I WROTE A BOOK in 2019 about President Trump and all the ways he lies about his golf scores, his golf "championships," his golf skills, his golf courses, his golf wealth, and his golf handicap. It was called Commander in Cheat. *Some loved it. Some hated it like a paper cut in the eye.*

I was promoting it on an NPR radio show hosted by two women and a man. I was in a remote room on the East Coast somewhere (you know, book tours) and they were in San Francisco and nothing was landing. I felt like I was talking to Easter Island statues. Maybe my mic was off?

Finally, I said something like, "If you guys get any more excited about this interview, I think I might get frostbite."

One Woman: It's just that we all hate golf.

The Guy: We think it's elitist.

The Other Woman: And it's so white. It's sooo not diverse at all. And those clothes!

They all laughed.

I asked if any of them actually played golf. None did.

I said, "Well, if you tried it, you might like it. It's actually not elitist. Ninety-one percent of golf rounds are played on public courses. The average cost for a round is $32. It's a great way to be with your friends, get some fresh air, exercise. And it's really, really fun."

There was a scoff, some sniffing, and about five seconds of dead air. That's about when they went to a piece on the plight of Chechen blanket weavers.

I don't mind. I'm happy to defend golf. I know too many ways it's changed people's lives.

————————

The Six-Foot Golf Course

At the Hanoi Hilton, the infamous North Vietnamese POW prison, the guards had 1,000 rules—no talking, no reading, no signals—all punishable by three days in the stocks.

But in 1965, when they threw American reconnaissance pilot Colonel George Hall into his seven-by-six-foot isolation cell, they had no rule against what he was about to do.

Play golf.

It started when he found a stick one day during his half hour of exercise by himself in the yard. He hid it up his pants leg. After that, he'd get up each morning and pick the course for the day. It might be Pebble Beach. Might be Pine Valley. Often it was his own Hattiesburg (Mississippi) Country Club. Every day, for his nearly four years in isolation, Hall would get his golf shoes on, kiss his wife, drive to the club, wave at everybody in town, say hello to the shoeshine guy, kid the pro a little, and walk to the first tee.

He'd take a couple of waggles with the stick and then make his easy-tempo swing. He'd watch it sail. Since he usually hit a driver back home about 240 yards, he'd pace off 240 yards in that cell—about 100 trips from one end to the other. He'd find the ball and—wait! There's Mrs. Hindmiller!

"Good morning, Mrs. Hindmiller," he'd say aloud. "Lovely day." Pause. "What's that?" Pause. "Might rain today? Uh-oh,

Pat's gonna be on me to fix the roof!" And then he'd wave and walk on.

"Sometimes a guard would open the shutter and watch me," Hall wrote in his book *Commitment to Honor*. "He just shook his head and made a gesture like I was crazy."

But Colonel Hall wasn't crazy. He was trying to keep from *going* crazy.

"[The guard] could never understand how much relief, if not pleasure, those rounds gave me," Hall wrote. "They gave me many hours of mentally being *outside* of that jail."

Before Vietnam, golf and Hall had been lifelong friends. A scratch handicap, he was the captain of the US Naval Academy golf team. Then the "police action" in Vietnam got him assigned to a squadron in Okinawa, Japan. In September of 1965, he was flying deep into enemy territory to photograph some bridge damage when he took ground flak, the plane caught fire, and he ejected.

It was two years before his family knew if he was living or dead. His injuries from the crash went untended. He fought dysentery, infections, boils, and vision loss. Those imaginary rounds of golf let him exercise his body and his mind. And what did he shoot? "Even par, always even par," he'd say.

After seven years, four months, and 18 days, he was released. He left home at 170 pounds. He was now 100. He came home sick and weak—but himself. When he landed in Hattiesburg, hundreds greeted him. He stepped to the podium and saw all those wonderful faces he'd seen in his rounds in his cell—the guy at the grocery store, the lady at the clothes shop, even Mrs. Hindmiller. He thanked each of them for unwittingly helping him get through it.

He went home to find he was still Pat's husband, still father to his three kids, despite how much they'd grown in seven years. "He talked about those rounds he'd play in his cell," says the oldest son, Bobby, now a golf pro. "It wasn't just the golf. It was all the people he'd see. It was his tool for keeping sane."

What's also amazing is that all that imaginary golf actually kept his game together. "He came home with that same rhythmic Payne Stewart type swing," Bobby marvels. In fact, within a month of his return, he was invited to play by an old friend—the newly crowned 1969 US Open champion, Sergeant Orville Moody. Hall shot 81 and Moody 76.

Colonel George Hall went back to his life. He became an executive for Coca-Cola, ran for Congress, and chaired the local United Way. But he was happiest playing the game that saved his mind. He lived a long, full life. At 83, Hall died with a trophy case of military awards pinned to his chest.

In 2015, my wife and I visited the Hanoi Hilton—where both Hall and the late senator John McCain were held—and were gobsmacked at how tiny, dark, and cold the cells were. And it hit me that it must've taken a very big mind to turn those 42 square feet of hell into sunshine.

The Heckler

Only in golf can thousands of people stand and watch two athletes battle to the final moment and not so much as sneeze. Can you imagine the World Series, Game 7, bottom of the ninth, two outs, bases loaded, and all the fans being as quiet as an oil painting?

That's why it was so shocking what happened that fall day in

2019 at the Visa Open de Argentina. It was the third playoff hole. Long-bombing American pro Brandon Matthews took his putter back on a very makable eight-foot uphill putt. Suddenly, out of the thundering silence came a huge guttural shriek.

Matthews flinched and missed the putt badly, short and left, costing him not just the tournament, but a pile of pesos and a possible spot in the Open Championship. He spun toward the sound and threw his arms up, the universal symbol for "What the hell, man?"

"I thought it was intentional," Matthews remembers.

Screaming on somebody's shot is utterly taboo in golf. No wonder people instantly turned toward the screamer and glared at him, open-mouthed. *How dare you?*

Matthews was devastated. He stared at his feet, looked back at the noise, shook the winner's hand, went back into the locker room, slumped into a chair, and called his dad. "You're not gonna believe what just happened," he said. "I had an easy uphill putt to tie the third playoff hole and somebody yelled—right on my backswing!"

But that's when a tournament official named Claudio Rivas approached. He had an explanation. He said the man who yelled had Down syndrome and only shrieked because of the tension and excitement in the air. It wasn't intentional. The man didn't even understand what he was doing.

That's when Brandon Matthews did a crazy thing. He said, "Take me to him."

Take you to him?

"Right now."

They went back on the course and found the man. His name was Juanchi. He was short and a little pudgy, about 40 years old, with curly red-brown hair under a yellow baseball cap. He was with his parents. The 6-4, 210-pound Matthews came directly at him.

Uh-oh.

And that's when Matthews grinned and...opened his arms.

Juanchi came running at Matthews with a giant smile and hugged him like a long-lost brother. Matthews gave him a signed glove and ball and told him, thru Rivas, he was SO glad he came out to the tournament today and there were no hard feelings and he hoped he had fun.

Wait. What?

"It wasn't his fault," Matthews says. "I didn't want him to have a bad taste in his mouth about the day. He could've really been upset by what happened and I wanted him to know everything was fine. I told him I hoped he stayed a golf fan for his whole life."

Where does somebody find that kind of forgiveness? That kind of humanity? That kind of empathy for a complete stranger? Matthews found it growing up. His childhood best friend had a sister with Down syndrome. His own mom worked in group homes with Down syndrome patients. Brandon Matthews wasn't taught just how to deal with the mentally challenged, he was taught how to love them.

"These people have so much love in them," he says. "There's no fake emotions with them. They just come at you with pure joy. You can see it on their face. There's no hiding it."

When Matthews got back to the locker room, feeling much better about life, his buddy said, "Dude, this is going to start a buzz. Stuff is going to happen from this."

"What's gonna happen?" Matthews scoffed. "We're in Argentina. I'm still going to finish second. Nothing's gonna happen."

Oh, but it did. The story of the Golfer Who Hugged the Fan Who Cost Him the Tournament started getting around. The Golf Channel. NBC. All the golf websites. Arnold Palmer's Bay Hill tournament was so impressed with Brandon, it gave him a tournament exemption.

The best part of it all has been the letters from parents of children with Down syndrome, which keep on coming. "It's not easy for some of these parents, how their children are treated," Matthews says. "I remember one said something like, 'Brandon, I want to thank you for what you've done. You've shown people how to treat people like my son. It means so much to us.'"

When the strongest among us help the weakest, it lifts everybody, doesn't it?

Juanchi and his parents are now big believers in the Book of Matthews. They send him inspirational quotes and go-get-'em texts. He needs it. Working your way up from golf's minor leagues to the Big Show isn't easy. But with a swing speed that matches Bryson DeChambeau's and a short game sharp as a Ginsu knife, a lot of people in golf think he can do great things.

Me, I think he already has.

Keiser Roll

Remember those cute, funny Sandra Boynton animal birthday cards we all used to buy? There was one I remember. On the outside, a hippo was next to a bluebird that was next to two sheep. Then the caption: "Hippo Birdie Two Ewe."

Ms. Boynton sold millions of birthday cards for the little Recycled Paper Greetings card company, so many that the owner, a man named Mike Keiser, was able to sell it for the GNP of Belgium, quit entirely, and start building some of the greatest golf courses in the world.

Here's just a few: Pacific Dunes (ranked 17th in the United States by *Golf Digest*); Bandon Dunes (37th); Old Macdonald (56th); Bandon Trails (67th); Sand Valley (112th); Mammoth Dunes (152nd); Cabot Cliffs, Nova Scotia (11th in the outside-the-United States rankings); Cabot Links, Nova Scotia (35th); and his coming attraction—maybe the best of all—Cabot Saint Lucia in the Caribbean. Mike Keiser is the best thing to happen to golf since the Big Bertha.

"When we started out in the greeting card business, we were grossing $1 million," Keiser says. "Once we got Sandra, we ended up at $100 million."

Thank you, Sandra, for giving golf the very humble genius Mike Keiser and all the great stuff he stands for: walking golf, play-the-land-under-your-feet golf, public golf, buddy-trip golf you'll remember for a lifetime.

"I love Mike Keiser," says Boynton, who made the first ace ever on the 12th hole at Bandon Dunes. "He really is a genius. But he won't tell you that. It's always somebody else that deserves the credit, not him."

Before Keiser, golf was in the Bloatozoic Era, when every good course was only accessible to fat old white guys with the $100,000 it took to join. The Experience at Visa Acres. That kind of thing. They were all set behind big gold gates and had quarter-mile treks between greens and tees, crossable only by a fully charged golf cart. At a Keiser course, you can't even *find* a cart.

"If the cart didn't ruin American golf, it ruined a lot of it," Keiser says. "I can't stand courses you can't walk." Even in his early 70s, Keiser is still thin as a ball retriever and can walk 36 holes a day.

I love Keiser because he gave us caddies again, maybe because he was a caddy himself growing up outside Buffalo. He gave us tee boxes right next to greens again, not to mention stunning holes that flirt with ocean cliffs and inland dunes, carved by nature not a Caterpillar.

I say this with the utmost respect, but if you were to play a round with Keiser, you would be wildly unimpressed. He goes out of his way to seem like any other chap. His clothes were cool 20 years ago. His son has had to work every job at Bandon, including caddy and fairway mower. Keiser's woods don't even have headcovers. Last time I was at Bandon, my caddy told me that Keiser's 5 wood has a split in the shaft. "We can get you a new one at the turn," the caddy said.

"No way," Keiser said. "I'm playing this one until it breaks."

Every one of his jaw-dropping 18-holers are public. "I was in Scotland playing once," says Keiser, who competed collegiately at Amherst. "And I noticed that on every single course, you could call up and get a tee time. They're happy to have you."

I love Keiser because he brought back the what-the-hell-let's-do-it! golf trip. His Bandon Dunes golf resort is voted No. 1 golf resort in the world every year. Imagine that: Better than Pinehurst. Better than Pebble Beach. Better than St. Andrews. Oh, and light years better than anything Trump has built, even though Trump said—get this—that Bandon Dunes is a "toy compared to" his Trump Los Angeles, which a) isn't in Los Angeles and b) isn't ranked anywhere on any national list, even the ones that go to 200.

I call Keiser the anti-Trump. Trump's courses represent everything I hate in golf: gold toilets and 100-foot waterfalls that spring out of nowhere and signs warning you to stay the hell out.

"I've never once thought to ask an architect, 'Hey, build me a 100-foot waterfall, OK?'" Keiser says.

You ever play a Trump course?

"No."

Ever met him?

"I'd rather not. That's kind of a life goal."

You know Trump hates you.

"I'm kinda proud of that."

My kind of guy.

Fast Company

You have no idea the sacrifices I make for you people.

Take speedgolf. This is the taking of a sport a lot of people hate and making it worse.

"No," says Wesley Cupp, a world champion speedster. "We took golf and made it into a sport."

OK, that's fine, if your idea of sport is to tee off at 5:30 a.m.

and play golf like you're double parked and be done by 6:30 so you can get back, shower up, and be at work at 8. But isn't that the whole point of golf, to miss all that?

"I hear that a lot," says Garlin Smith, the head of Speedgolf SoCal in LA. "My buddies say, 'Garlin, you're killing me. I need my wife to think Saturday golf takes eight hours.'"

Just thinking about speedgolf makes me tired. US champ Scott Dawley won the 2020 title by shooting a 75 in 43 minutes for a speedgolf score of 118 (75 + 43 = 118). Does that sound... fun?

But, for you, I agreed to try it.

We met at 5:15 a.m. (I mean, *Jesus*) at Chester Washington Golf Course in LA. By "we" I mean "insane chisel-faced fitness freaks" who make up Speedgolf SoCal, and me. The starter at Chester Washington lets them go sprinting off first about 15 minutes before the sun rises. For the first hole or two, they use glow balls.

I drove slit-eyed while I scarfed down a breakfast Hot Pocket and made it just in time. In the parking lot, I met Smith and hated him immediately. He was a 56-year-old surfer who looked 46. Worse, he kept talking about how much fun I was about to have. "Speedgolf is perfect to keep your game sharp," he said in his annoying happy way. "Get in some cardio and get on with life's requirements."

I had a question: *Why are we doing this again?*

"Because you're going to feel so great getting in your car, having worked out and played 18 holes while cars are just pulling up to start their round."

Meh.

Speedgolf is like regular golf. You have to wait until the ball stops rolling and putt everything out and rake the bunkers. But it's not like regular golf. You wear workout gear. You carry a streamlined golf bag with no more than six clubs, though some only carry a 6 iron. If the ball goes out-of-bounds, you drop along the line of flight and hit. There's no three-minute search rule. There's barely a three-second rule. Also, there's no time for the honor system. Some holes, everybody is hitting at once.

Well, it all sounded just delightful to me.

My threesome included Garlin and a lawyer whose body seemed to suggest that he'd never run after a bus, much less a golf ball. "I do this because I hate slow play," Randy Balik said. "I mean, do you think I got a body like this because I like *running*?"

But the instant he hit his first drive, he was off like he'd just robbed a liquor store. Before I could absorb it, Garlin had hit and was off, too, which meant I was playing golf in a jailbreak. Swinging at the speed of light, I swiped it miles right. Since I didn't have a glow ball, it was surely lost. I quickly teed up another and hit it nearly the same exact place.

Q: When can an hour feel like a week?
A: Playing speedgolf.

I noticed most of these guys were wearing two rain gloves because they sweat so much. "You think a four footer is tough?" Cupp wrote me. "Try it with your heart beating out of your chest as sweat pours off your nose and onto the ball. And then do it again for 17 more holes."

I was running as fast as my 63-year-old asthmatic lungs would take me and so I'd try to make up for lost time by swinging really fast and really hard, sweat stinging my eyes, hitting pig slices and snipe hooks, which only added time zigzagging across the course, while Randy and Garlin were zipping along in straight lines.

Somewhere in the misery it hit me all the dumb things I'd done. I'd worn sunglasses. (The sun was barely up.) I'd put a scorecard in my pocket. (You keep your score in your head.) I had two ball markers. (Nobody marks anything.)

By the time I got to the sixth tee, the speed group in front of us was already on 8. Randy kept checking his watch.

After nine holes, I could feel that Hot Pocket trying to stage a comeback. (Oddly, it tasted the same either way.) I was done, spent, finished. Smith saw my failure coming way ahead of time and had a golf cart ready at the turn. I've never been happier to get into one in my life. My nine-hole time was 45 minutes, about 10 minutes slower than these guys usually go and god knows what I'd shot. I'd lost count. Maybe 45? Over 18 holes, that would've been a speedgolf score of 180.

The guy driving the cart was named Jason Vaughan, a really good player whose best normal round is 5 under and best speed round is 2 under.

He said his hero was Wes Cupp. "He's like a god to us," said Vaughan, who was nursing an injury. "His transition time is like six seconds." Turns out "transition time" is the time it takes to switch from running to hitting to running again, a kind of golfing pit stop. Cupp is famous for putting with his bag hanging off a carabiner hooked to his waist. He's the Steve Jobs of speedgolf.

Freed from their anchor (me), Randy and Garlin played the back nine in 34 minutes. That's not even four minutes per hole. I know guys who plumb-bob for four minutes. For some reason (me), they'd given up keeping score, but I'm guessing without this handicap (me), they'd each have shot about 78 in 68 minutes, for an SG score of 146. Strong.

I didn't entirely hate it. Speedgolf taught me some cool things about golf that I didn't know before.

1. Practice swings are useless. To a man, the speedgolfers all said they shoot about the same playing speedgolf (no practice swings) as they do normal golf (many practice swings.) I've been wasting years of my life.
2. Fourteen clubs aren't necessary. After playing speedgolf, I now take out my 4 iron and lob wedge when I'm carrying my bag. Hasn't made a lick of difference and my shoulders thank me.
3. Yardage watches are a godsend. The speedos all wear them because they save so much time. If every golfer in America wore a yardage watch, the world would be a happier place.

But I knew I'd never speedgolf again, for three reasons:

1. The bullsh*t. Eighty-two percent of the joy of golf for me is giving the needle to my buddies, telling stories, and recapping the glory and sorrow of the last hole.

Ted: I think my wife could've played that hole better than you and she's never played.

Me: Maybe. I'll ask her tomorrow morning after you leave for work.

All that's gone in speedgolf. You can't needle your buddies because they're always off leaping over a bush somewhere.

2. The job of it. The FunMeter needle is at about 1/16th in speedgolf. It's more like timing yourself cleaning out the garage. You feel good about it when you're done, but the same can be said for flossing.

And, the ultimate dealbreaker...

3. No beer.
   You think I got a body like this because I like Gatorade?

Sol Goldberg

For a lot of us, it's not the perfect 7 iron that keeps us coming back, or the monthly birdie, or even the cold Budweisers. It's the slightly out-of-round families we make among the people we play with, come 69 or 109.

Take our family friend, Sol Goldberg, a workaday Colorado golf pro who used to give my dad an occasional lesson. Sol was a muni pro, though he looked more like a visiting Russian professor. He was dignified, tall with a deep voice, and always had a pipe in his hand.

He also had a permanent hole in his wallet. He wasn't broke because of golf. He was broke because of a dice game called barbudi. Sol was to barbudi what Willy Loman was to sales. Whenever there was big money in the barbudi pot, poor Sol's luck always seemed to have jumped on the 51 crosstown bus.

Sol just barely got by. He roomed with his brother next to the A&W in Boulder. He was a pro, so he could take you to the Monday Pro-Ams but it was understood that you paid all his expenses. When you beat him out of a $20, you half wondered if he'd eat that night, which didn't seem right for someone who'd fought in Italy during WWII.

After he retired, he became part of my brother's band of daily bandits known as the Goon Squad. Sol would play with them every day—sun or snow—and whatever he might win on the golf course, he'd usually lose, and then some, on barbudi. But the older Sol got, the more his golf dwindled. His chip yips got so bad the Goons would look away, since everybody knows the yips are contagious.

One day, one of Sol's buddies reported that Sol couldn't even watch Broncos games anymore because his TV was broken. The Goons decided then and there to chip in and buy him a new one. But it hit one of the Goons that Sol would be hurt worse by the charity than by the thing itself. Generally, a Goon would rather walk 100 miles barefoot through carpet tacks than admit he doesn't have money for shoes. Forget that idea.

A month or so later, it so happened there was a Goons-only raffle—$10 a ticket. First prize: a brand-new flat-screen TV. Most guys bought five or ten tickets. Sol scraped up enough to buy one. That day, after the day's 18-hole combat, each Goon sat clutching his ticket in his closed fists. The Head Goon reached into the hat, looked at the ticket, and announced, "Sol Goldberg!" They say you could've seen Sol's smile from downtown Denver.

In the parking lot, Sol tied the TV down in the trunk of his old broken-down Buick, waved triumphantly to the rest of the Goons, and drove off.

Not one Goon ever told him that Sol's name was written on every ticket.

WANDERER

I'VE BEEN WORKING ON this next piece for over 30 years.

See, I'm a travel freak and a golf freak, so in 1990, I had this idea to combine them for Sports Illustrated. *I told them I'd like to go play the 18 most unforgettable holes in the world. And not just that, I'd play them in order—the most unforgettable first hole in the world, the most unforgettable second hole, etc., and by the end, I'd have a score for playing the whole unforgettable enchilada.*

Get this: they let me.

I went around the world in three weeks, doing nothing but playing golf. Starting in Denver and—note to Flat Earthers—always flying east, I went to New York, Ireland, Scotland, South Africa, Dubai, Thailand, Indonesia, Japan, Australia, Hawaii, Los Angeles, and back to Denver. At every stop, they just couldn't wait to show me the hole they thought was unforgettable-worthy.

"Ah, but maybe I should probably play them all, just in case, right?" I'd say.

"But of course!" they'd say.

God, was that fun. But every time I'd try to carve out time to write it, my editors would give me something else to write first. Then I'd hear about some other piece of unforgettableness and have to go play it. Then the golf-nut managing editor quit and the tennis-nut editor took over and I was there for 16 more years and I never got to write it.

Until now...

The Unforgettable 18

1. Handara, Bali, Indonesia

You might play Handara for the Tarzan beauty of a course carved out of an extinct volcano crater, an engineering marvel built by hundreds of villagers moving the earth out of the jungle in baskets.

You might play Handara for the shimmering lakes or the mountain peaks wearing clouds as hats. Or the women groundskeepers walking with shovels balanced on their heads.

You might even play Handara for its sheer remoteness. I remember checking into the elegant hotel late in the afternoon before my round and calling the front desk.

Me: What time's dinner?
Operator: What time would you like it?
Me: Excuse me?
Operator: Sir, you are the only guest in the rooms.

Me, I play Handara for the monkeys. Most especially the monyet monkeys on the par 5 first that are famous for hopping down out of the trees and stealing your ball. Well, I was *told* they would, but it didn't happen when I played it the first time, on my way to making a par.

Since I was staying there, I went back later in the day and hit another approach shot to the green. No monkey. Third time— yes! A cute little thief pounced on it and scampered back up the banana tree with it.

Nobody's ever figured out what they do with all those balls. I've spent an inordinate amount of time fantasizing about it. My hope is that one day some fat tycoon is putting on that green when, suddenly, every monkey starts firing balls at his head, knocking him out cold.

2. The National, Cape Schanck, Australia

Nobody wants to play a course with the word *shank* in it, but you need to see this cliffside ocean beauty. It's a 155-yard par 3 stunner that isn't just breathtaking, it's life-taking.

On the beach just under this hole, the sitting prime minister of Australia, Harold Holt, drowned on December 17, 1967. That day, Holt, 59, finished up work in Canberra and drove his maroon Pontiac down to Cheviot Beach at Cape Schanck. Holt was a scuba diver, spear fisherman, and rough-water swimmer, so much so that during cabinet meetings, he'd secretly hold his breath to improve his submerge time. That afternoon, he dove into the roiling water alone and disappeared.

Because his body was never found, all kinds of theories have been dreamed up about what "really" happened to him:

1. Holt swam underwater to a hidden spot around the rocks, where his mistress picked him up and drove off.

2. A Chinese submarine, waiting offshore, kidnapped him.
3. "I reckon the sharks got him," theorized my Aussie playing partner.

Playing this hole reminds Aussies of all of that, which is just a little macabre. Can you imagine Americans playing a golf hole on top of the Texas School Book Depository?

3A. Mauna Kea, the Big Island, Hawaii

This hole is like Angelina Jolie—gorgeous, long, and a little too hard. It's the show-stoppingest par 3 in the South Pacific, with a green perched above the most splendid beach in all of Hawaii.

In fact, this hole is so long that when owner Laurance Rockefeller put up $50,000 winner-take-all in 1964 for the Big Three (Nicklaus, Palmer, and Gary Player) to play a four-day tournament, Player saw the back tee at 272 yards and threatened to go home. He couldn't get it across even with a driver. "Well how would *you* like to come to the 3rd hole and not get to the 4th?" he asked. They moved it up.

You can't really play that tee anymore but I snuck back there anyway and rinsed a sleeve trying to do what Player couldn't. They say a guy from Cypress Point stayed a week and tried every sunset to do it. He used up 20 balls a day until he finally made it on the seventh. And then he rested.

I hit my actual shot from 180 yards—a knifed 4 iron that was lucky to reach the front bunker and earn me a bogey I richly deserved. Then I walked down to that perfect beach and saw a nest of giant green turtles, while the waves spritzed my face and a hint of jasmine sauntered by.

And I thought, *no way* Gary Player was going home.

3B. Punta Mita, Mexico

OK, this is really The Unforgettable 19, as you can see, because of The Hole Jack Nicklaus Forgot to Build. See, he'd built the course the first time through and was happy with it. But when he came back to play in the grand opening, he came to the third hole and slapped his forehead. He'd completely whiffed on the best hole of all.

"It was just sitting there," Nicklaus told me. "It was a perfect par 3 and I never saw it." So he built it anyway, a one-in-a-million hole, 180 yards, par 3, to a perfect island. Just stuck out in the sea, an island, and you have to hit it. After your tee shot, you climb into a six-wheel amphibious vehicle. Most times, it's a boat, except at low tide, when it's a kind of mudcat jeep.

Unlike the floating, mechanical par 3 green at Coeur d'Alene in Idaho, this island is all natural, only a few rocks off the back of the green were built to keep people from taking 90 minutes to finish. (With 19 holes to play at Punta Mita, you need to pick up the pace.) By the way, if you ace 3B, tradition dictates you have to swim to the green. Me, I made a lovely birdie 2 there, a 3B2, if you will.

Punta Mita is big with honeymooners. One late afternoon, a couple snuck onto the island to screw and by the time they were done, the tide had risen and they had to be rescued.

Like I say, at 3B, it's better to be quick.

4. Lahinch, County Clare, Ireland

I played this Alister MacKenzie gem—a blind par 5—only once and it's hard to say which part of the day I loved more.

Was it the goat that followed us all 18 holes? Turns out that's not unusual at Lahinch. There's a statue of a goat outside the clubhouse.

Was it that we played the fourth in freezing sideways rain and yet when we looked behind us, there were a few hundred surfers in the water? In Ireland. My buddy Skybox was amazed and said to the caddy, "There's gotta be 200 surfers back there!" To which the caddy said matter-of-factly, "Ah, 'tis a nice day for it."

Was it that our approach to the green was not only blind, and not only over a towering dune, but required us to wait until a little man came out from a little hovel and waved a green flag? It's true. In squalls like this one, he scrambles out of a small shelter dug into the far side of the dune, waves a red flag, and scurries back in. Then, when the green is clear, he crawls out again and waves a green one. The members call him "George the Fourth."

Or was it that after we tipped our caddy, we saw him inside the clubhouse, drinking at the bar? Turns out the caddies are all members. Hell, maybe the goats are, too?

Answer: Yes.

5. Teeth of the Dog, Casa de Campo, Dominican Republic

Near the tee box of this par 3, a little guy was selling used balls out of a basket. There was another, even littler guy. He spoke to us in English.

"You want ball?" the guy said.

"Sorry?" I said.

He pointed to the guy with the basket and said, "He sell. You buy. You hit. He find. He sell. You buy." He couldn't hide the shadow of a grin on his face. Some racket.

It was such an honest pitch, I bought some balls. Then I got up to look at the hole and figured out why these guys had such a good business. It might be the only golf hole with no land. It's a par 3 that's 98% water. There's a little spit of land that pretends to be a tee box and a little kitchen-table-sized green that barely pokes its head out of the jungle. The rest is all bay and fish and the sound of your knees knocking.

Somehow, I hit a good one. It wound up 15 feet from the hole, which I'd two-putt for a par. I looked over at the two little guys. They seemed disappointed.

6. Navatanee, Bangkok, Thailand

Thai service is always impeccable, but at this place, they treat you like you're Vishnu. For instance, when I got to the practice range, I was given three caddies.

"Three caddies?" I asked my host, Dr. "Suki" Navapan. He replied, "The king of Malaysia get four. You not king."

The three caddies were all head to toe in blue and yellow with giant winged Flying Nun hats and white sun cream all over their faces. To be tan in Thailand is to be judged a farmworker.

Caddy 1's job was to actually caddy, but her style was unique. She'd hurry to the ball in the fairway, pick it up, clean it, and throw it back down, a perfectly illegal move. Same on greens. Pick it up, wash it, throw it down, no mark. Not a stickler for the rules, Caddy 1.

Caddy 2's job was to hold a sun umbrella over my head.

Caddy 3's job was to drive the cart, which I never rode in. This distressed 1, 2, and 3 very much. "Car! Car! Car!" they kept saying, pointing to the empty passenger seat.

Suki must've been a very powerful man because foursomes

in front of us kept pulling over so we could play through, even though we hadn't asked. I made a mental note:

Do not beat Suki. You might wake up in the morning next to a cobra.

The sixth was sensational—a long par 4 that flirted constantly with lakes and flowering trees and a river that flowed along the side until it suddenly cut across the fairway 260 yards out. Sadly, I made a Jackson Pollock out of it, hitting one lake and one bunker on the way to a 7.

Afterward, Suki said if I gave the caddies $5 each they'd be over the moon. I gave them $10.

Me king.

7. Pole Creek, Winter Park, Colorado

"You either love 7," says Pole Creek's manager, Mary Moynihan, "or you hate it."

I love it. It's the only 180-degree U-turn hole I've ever heard of. It's also the only par 5 I've ever heard of where you can drive the green. To do that, though, you have to turn sideways and hit it over towering lodgepole pines. I've never been able to do it and I've never seen anybody do it.

"I used to know a guy who could do it," says Dale Freeman, a Pole Creeker. "You gotta hit it about 380 though." Of course, you're at the Continental Divide, so you're 8,700 feet up, which means the ball will travel 13 percent farther, so...maybe.

But...if you hit a tree, you're dead, because you'll hear it ricochet off trees for about 30 seconds and you'll never find it. Even going into those woods to look isn't a great idea, since this course is also the stomping grounds of moose. One Sunday morning as he walked to church, the ex-mayor of nearby Grand Lake got stomped to death by a moose. And even if you *are* able to fly the trees, if you miss the green left, then you're back on the sixth hole—the hole you just played—and it's OB. Local rule. They did that because guys like my friend Kevin Cartin figured out you could just hit an iron *backward* onto 6 and then an iron onto 7 and make a birdie and lots of enemies in the group behind you.

I took the conventional way—a draw over the far edge of the trees down to the front of the lake. From there, a mid-iron to a small island (I said the hole is crazy) and then an iron straight uphill to the smallest green on the course. Two-putt par.

This thing is like a stew my mom used to make. They've thrown everything in the kitchen into it and it turned out delicious.

8. Pebble Beach, Carmel, California

This is my favorite hole in the world and without doubt the greatest par 4 ever built. It's been featured in dozens of movies, including *Follow the Sun*, *The Parent Trap* (1961 version), and *The Sandpiper*. It has played the coast of France in *Bluebeard's 8th Wife*, the coast of England in *National Velvet*, and Pine Island, Maine, in *A Summer Place*. No wonder. It's at once stunning, unforgettable, and terrifying. It's this good: in its whole history, there's no record of anybody playing through on it. If you were in bed with Halle Berry, would you hurry?

All of Pebble is an eye-gasm, and not just for golfers. Marshals have to kick hikers off it every day and, once in a while, horseback riders. One time, the first group of the day came up 18 to find a Japanese family having a picnic in the greenside bunker.

But the eighth is not to be fooled with. You hit your 3 wood up to a nosebleed cliff and it's all you can do to peek over and straight down the perilous cliff to the rocky, wave-crushed cove below. There's a story about two Japanese golfers playing in the fog and driving straight off the cliff to their death, but I've never been able to confirm it. One lady *did* forget to set the brake on her cart and it rolled off the cliff and dropped the 150 feet to its rocky demise.

You see all manner of critters down there—sea lions, pelicans, and otters with clams on their chests whacking them with rocks. One day, a caddy was amazed to see a giant rock down below that wasn't there the day before. Then he realized it was a beached whale.

Take a minute and savor "the greatest second shot in golf," as Jack Nicklaus calls it. See the yawning crevasse you must cross to get to the tiny green, which barely hangs off the cliff. I'm a 6 handicap. I bet I've played it 20 times and I think I've had 18 bogeys, just as I did the first time I saw it. I just can't get it out of my head that if you miss that green right, it's heading for Hawaii. And yet, my son Jake, who is about a 13 handicap, parred it the only time he played it.

"Hard?" he said. "What hard?"

9. Ailsa, Turnberry, Scotland

I know, I know. This list has too many par 3s, but whose fault is that? This 248-yarder can't be left off. Yes, it was bought by Donald Trump in 2014 and I can't tell you how much this pains me to say this, but...he made this hole so much better.

Start with one of the greatest tee boxes in the world, a patch of nervous land surrounded by the crashing Irish Sea. You have to launch a 3 wood, at least, over all that rugged beauty, with ocean up the side and a postcard yellow-and-white lighthouse in the background. I bailed out right, chipped on, and was happy with a bogey.

That lighthouse was built by the family of Robert Louis Stevenson. I've been up in the balcony there and it's thrilling. The middle level is a gorgeous suite for the Turnberry hotel, which lords elegantly over the course. The bottom level is now a snack shack, where you can eat your awful cucumber sandwich, sit on the lovely porch, and watch Ailsa Craig in the distance.

It would be the greatest rest stop in all of golf if not for...

Halfway House—El Tamarindo, Puerto Vallarta, Mexico

There's only one problem with this little snack shack that sits half a lob wedge above a crashing inlet: it stops play cold.

Sitting on the porch, with the Pacific splashing under your FootJoys, you dab yourself with iced lemongrass-scented towels and watch whales cavort in the distance. You wonder if anybody would mind if you'd just sit there the rest of the afternoon. Then, when you taste the fresh ceviche and the freshly grilled octopus, you stop caring what they'd think.

One time we just couldn't bear to leave it, so we told the group behind us, "Hey, go ahead and play through. We're gonna sit here a little longer."

And the guy said, "Can't help you. That's what *we're* going to do."

10. Bel Air, Los Angeles, California

The late Jim Murray, sports columnist for the *Los Angeles Times*, had nothing but trouble with this famous swinging-bridge par 3. It's 220 yards and the carry over the yawning barranca in front is at least 175. Jim was the best sportswriter who ever lived, but he may have been the worst golfer. He'd had two childhood diseases and had only one good eye, and even the bad eye could see that for him to hit it over the barranca would be a miracle.

So before he hit, Jim would take an old ball out of his bag and heave it into the chasm. Then he'd turn to his befuddled playing partners and say, "An appeasement to the gods."

When you play it the first time—I made a bogey—and cross the elegant bridge, you're charmed by the sheer lightness of it, as though you're crossing into Brigadoon. One time, the comedian Tom Poston (the bumbling Vermont handyman in *Newhart*) was walking over it when somebody yelled, "Hey, Tommy! Why don't you bungee jump off that thing?"

Poston turned and, without a beat, yelled, "Nope. Came into this world on a busted rubber, not going out on one."

11. Pine Valley, New Jersey

There's a thing known as "pure" in golf. A brand-new white Titleist 1 is pure. An orange Kirkland 8 embossed with "THIS AIN'T YOUR BALL" is not. Walking with your bag at sunset is pure. Riding in a cart with a horn that plays the Texas fight song is not. A $5 Nassau: pure. Bingo Bango Bongo: not.

Everything about Pine Valley is pure. The humble little cottage you woke up in, the thump your 8 iron makes off those perfect fairways, your snapper soup with sherry for lunch. There's a reason Pine Valley is voted the #1 course in the world every year. It's all so...pure. This hole is my favorite because it feels like it was always there, just waiting for someone to stick a flag in it. It swoops and swerves, a dancing green sea.

The first time I played it, we had a caddy who could tell what kind of tree you hit by the sound. For instance, early on in the round, I airmailed one way right. "That sounded like oak," the caddy said. "I think we can find it."

A few holes later, I smother-toed one way left. "Maple, I think," he said. "I know where to look."

On this one, on my way to a double bogey, I jacked one righter than right. We all listened, heard the *thwack*, and looked at the caddy.

"Aluminum siding," he said. "I think you hit Mr. Miller's house."

12. Old Head, Kinsale, Ireland

This hole will make your heart race like police lights in your rearview mirror. It's the only green I've ever played that takes up an entire peninsula, so that each side of it falls off 250 feet to the thundering waves below. The land under you is so narrow there are actual tunnels through it, carved by wind and water, so that you can watch a bird fly under you on one side and come out on the other.

There's a sign: *Do Not Pass. Five Feet Further and You're Dead.*

It's so steep on the edges that one Irishman got vertigo and had to crawl in. "One?" says owner and cofounder Patrick O'Connor. "Dozens. Happens quite regularly."

It's a par 5 with a section the caddies call Haulie's Leap, for the bulldozer driver who was helping shape the tee when his dozer started leaning, causing Haulie to leap out and the dozer to tumble all the way down to the pitiless rocks. It's still down there.

As you get ready to hit your terrifying drive, it's hard to forget that Old Head is accustomed to disaster. This is the last land the passengers of the *Titanic* might have seen before it sunk in 1912. It's also not far from where the Germans sank the *Lusitania* in 1915. So you hit and hope and it's all so fun the caddies let you hit a provisional, just because. I was delighted with my par.

By the way, as you turn toward 13 tee, you'll see the still-working lighthouse off 18. A few years back, the keeper had two wives, one Irish and one Estonian.

As I mentioned, at Old Head, provisionals are allowed.

13. Lost City, Sun City, South Africa

I picked this hole for the alligators. There's an entire pit of them you have to hit over. It's a downhill par 3 of about 180 yards and the pit comes right up to the green.

There must be 30 alligators in there. There's a 10-foot sheer wall that keeps them from climbing up to eat you, but the edge of the green falls straight into the pit, which means you can be lining up a putt while the alligators are lining up you.

I have no agreement with the alligators, so I bailed out miles from them and bogeyed the hole. Personally, I hope they all became purses.

14. Composite, Royal Melbourne, Australia

Alister MacKenzie designed three masterpieces: Augusta, Cypress Point, and Royal Melbourne, a top-ten course in the world with beauty, intrigue, and, most of all, beautiful bunkers.

Ben Crenshaw came here and took 300 pictures of the bunkers. They're huge and interlocking and have lips big enough to make Mick Jagger jealous. If you're going, practice your bunker shots for about a month and then do it for three more months and you'll be ready.

This par 5 is such a blast you feel like you're doing something illegal. Even the plants on it are fun to say: eggs-and-bacon daisy, spike wattle, kangaroo grass, and chocolate lily. The tee box is under a gum tree. Standing on it, all you see are the three huge bunkers on the hill you must carry with your blind drive. Then the hole changes its mind and doglegs quickly to the right and downhill. Finally, you'll have to deal with nine bunkers around the green, the one on the left being the approximate size of the Rose Bowl.

Maybe the Aussie I was playing with knew how much I loved it all because he gave me a while to soak it all in and then said, "Good hole this, right?"

15. Augusta National, Georgia

If you have only one day at the Masters, spend it all in the bleachers behind 15, the most dangerous, tantalizing tease of a par 5 ever devised. Every kind of glory and heartache happens here, sometimes back to back.

Gene Sarazen won the second Masters here with maybe the greatest single shot in golf history—a 4 wood from 230 yards into the hole for an albatross or, as Sarazen called it, a "dodo." Curtis Strange blew the 1985 Masters on 15, then Seve Ballesteros did the same the next year. In 2013, Tiger Woods hit a stone-cold perfect wedge here, except it smacked the pin and bounced into the water, a situation made worse when Tiger, like a dodo, took an illegal drop, which caused him to drop four shots, which is exactly what he lost by. Sergio Garcia opened the defense of his 2017 title by dunking five different balls in the water, making a 13. "I made a 13 and never missed a shot," he said, which is the most Sergio thing ever.

I've played it probably 10 times, but only the first one counts and I made a hard-earned par, for which Tiger might've given me his yacht.

But the craziest thing that ever happened at 15 involved my nephew. It was after Tiger's epic win in 1997. My name was drawn out of a hat of media types to play the course that Monday. The problem was I had an afternoon flight out of Atlanta I couldn't miss. My brother was with me, so I said, "You caddy for me on the front nine, then I'll sneak off and you play the back. Nobody will know." On 15, he hit a particularly snazzy 9 iron and decided he'd save the divot to show his 12-year-old golf-crazy son, Travis.

But when he did, Travis grabbed it, took a bite out of it, and swallowed. Just like that.

"Now I'm *made* out of Augusta," he beamed.

16. Cypress Point, Pebble Beach, California

No golf calendar should be sold without this beauty. It's a par 3, 233 yards, and nearly every inch of it is carry, ocean, and sea lions. You play it in a headwind that would tip a cow over. That is, if you can ever stop taking pictures and actually swing.

My first time, I smashed a driver as hard as I could into the front bunker, then blasted out clumsily to 35 feet, then casually knocked it in for your basic 3. That's 13 shots better than the 16 Porky Oliver made on it once in the Crosby Clambake.

One year at the Crosby, pro Brett Upper's ball wound up on the beach below. He climbed down and was about to hit when his caddy yelled, "Hold up! Your amateur partner is about to play!" So Upper waited. While he was waiting, a rogue wave came and not only soaked him to the waist but took his ball away with it.

"I've had people come to this hole and walk in," our caddy said that day.

The hole was just too hard?

"No. They were out of balls."

One time I was playing it with Two Down O'Connor, the World's Most Avid Golf Gambler. He stood on the tee, turned sideways, and hit a 3 wood into the bailout fairway left.

"Two, what the hell are you doing?" I asked.

"What?" he argued. "That's my drive. It's right in the middle."

"Two, this is number 16, the famous par 3," I explained. "You have a big painting of this hole over your desk!"

"This is 16?"

Poor Two never got to play it again.

17. Cabot Saint Lucia, the Caribbean

OK, this is the exception to the rule. I've never played this par 3, but then, nobody has. It wasn't scheduled to open until 2023. But I flew over it in a helicopter and this thing is going to give your goosebumps goosebumps.

You'll tee off from a high rock, crossing over the blue blue ocean and the rocks and god knows what else to a puny little green on a skinny peninsula, 186 yards from you. "It's off-the-charts spectacular," says one half of the course's architects, Bill Coore of Coore & Crenshaw. "The waves are going to be crashing and you'll need to hit an incredible shot."

What's nuts is that the hole before it—the par 3 16th—is almost entirely ocean, too, which means Cabot Saint Lucia's back-to-back par 3 supermodels will rival the two best back-to-back par 3s in the world—15 and 16 at Cypress Point.

You might as well start figuring out how you're going to afford the flight there, because you're going to have to play it once in your life. Me, I was feeling loose and confident that day, so I'm giving myself a par.

No, I'm not taking any questions.

18. Old Course, St. Andrews, Scotland

The only reason we play 18 holes is because St. Andrews is 18 holes, and St. Andrews is 18 holes because the 18th green is where the old town of St. Andrews begins. There was no more room.

That's what makes 18 so wonderful. You go from the brutal Road Hole to the homeward-bound, open-armed 18th, a short par 4 that's as welcoming as a mother's homemade haggis.

The entire left side is the first hole. It's a double-wide fairway all the way to the first tee. And by the way, when the starter says, "Gentlemen, you're on the first tee," he means *the first tee*.

The entire right side is the town itself, including the old and handsome Rusacks Hotel. One time, a few of us writers rented a little house that literally touched the 18th fairway. I'd have my morning coffee watching people tee off on 1 and my afternoon tea watching them come down 18, happily taking pictures and spinning around like Mary Tyler Moore in downtown Minneapolis.

You hit your drive as far left as you want, then cross the most famous bridge in golf—the 700-year-old Swilcan—then try to hit the green without winding up in the diabolical Valley of Sin in front. It's a ball swallower, with humps and hollows that only old caddies can see.

The first time I played it, I was lining up a six-footer for birdie when I looked up to see at least 100 people leaning on the railing surrounding the green, watching me. One guy hollered, "Get it good and close, lad!" Another yelled, "Steady now!" Sadly, my putt took an unseen hump and I missed it. From the rail, I heard sympathetic groaning.

Coming off, I said to my Scottish playing partner: "That's so cool. They were rooting for me. This really is the home of golf."

"Nae," he said. "They hang on that rail all the day, betting each other on the putts. You probably cost somebody five pounds."

19th Hole. The Ryder Cup Bar, Kiawah, South Carolina

This was my Sophie's Choice. How could I not pick the Jigger Inn, just off the Road Hole at St. Andrews, with its cozy fireplace and happy people who've just played the most memorable round of their lives? How could I not choose Sticks, the firepit bar at Spanish Bay in Pebble, where I've drank many a delicious beer product serenaded by the bagpiper coming up the dunes? Or Castle Pines in Colorado, where the legendary clubhouse man, Tommy, could remember your name, drink, and wife's name even if you hadn't been there in three years?

I'll tell you how. Because the Kiawah 19th hole is so close to the 18th flag you feel like you're still on the green. You flop into your patio chair, exhausted by one of the most beautiful courses in the world, order up the scrumptious grilled cheese sandwich (with fried green tomatoes, pimento cheese, and ham on home-made corn bread), and toast each other to even finishing.

Let's do that now.

Cheers to The Unforgettable 18, which is really The Unforgettable 19. It took me thirty years to play. It's a par 73 and I shot an 83, took about a million pictures, flew tens of thousands of miles, made a hundred friends, a million memories, and met one monkey.

I hate to see it end. Just in terms of free golf, this was the single greatest boondoggle of an idea any golf writer ever dreamed up. My only regret is I never got to try the par 3 outside Lisbon that required you to hit over a major street (gone now), the hole in South Africa that requires you to take a chopper to the top of a 400-yard cliff, the one in Iceland made entirely of ice, the one—

Hey, wait a minute...Emergency nine?

Love-Love Golf

Some people prefer tofu over cheeseburgers, burlap over silk, Brahms over Beatles. I can live with that. But when they say they prefer tennis over golf, I want to stab two fondue forks into my ears.

Every tennis court, whether it's in New York or New Delhi, looks exactly the same. The net, the lines, even the benches, all the same, everywhere. (OK, you've got a few grass and clay courts. Be still my heart.) Every golf course, meanwhile, is different. Every golf hole is different. Do you realize there's an underwater hole in Australia? Ever see any underwater tennis courts?

Does tennis have stairs in play, like at Merion, outside Philadelphia? Do you know any tennis courts where you have to ring a bell after you're done, like on the blind par 3 at Cruden Bay near Aberdeen? Ride a funicular to get to the next hole, like at Industry Hills outside LA?

Some places in golf have outdoor elevators to get you to the next hole, like the one I played in Vermont. Some have old sheep gates you have to hit over, like at North Berwick. Do you remember Pete Sampras ever having to volley over a sheep gate?

When you finish a point in tennis, do you then have to walk down the charming main street of town and turn left at the bakery to get to the next shot, as happens in Irish golf? The best tennis can offer for charm is balls with fuzz on them.

In golf, you can be stuck behind a clump of ice plant with a fence post in your backswing, needing to hit a shot that has to fit under a rock outcropping, climb over a snack shack, and then get down before the lake. In tennis, you have to get it over the net.

In tennis, you can pay $2,500 to sit in the top row at Wimbledon to see the Match of the Century, Serena Williams vs. Naomi Osaka, which will be over in 51 minutes. In golf, you can pay $50 to see Tiger go head-to-head with Phil for four and a half hours, with each of them sometimes hitting shots so near you, you could knock off their hats.

I have one tennis-over-golf friend, who rejects all this. "Golf takes too long," he insists. "In tennis you can be done in an hour, hour and a half." To which I say, "Who wants to be done in an hour and a half? What's the big hurry to get home? Clean the gutters?"

"Pah!" he says. "Golf isn't even a workout. I can play a tennis match and it's a great workout." Not to Google you to death, but an hour and a half of tennis burns 900 calories. Most golfers walk 18 holes, which burns 1,500 calories, more if they carry.

What makes me love golf are 1,000 things and only a few are the actual playing the game itself. At the unbelievable moonscape of Sand Hills in Mullen, Nebraska, you land at the local airport and tell the guy at the rental counter you're there to play Sand Hills. He'll toss you a set of keys. No paperwork, no credit card, just the keys coming at you. You catch them and stick them in Old Smoky, a beat-up old wagon with dead bugs all over the window. You drive Old Smoky to Sand Hills, play some of the greatest golf of your life, drive Old Smoky back, and toss the guy the keys, making sure to never wash it, as per tradition. Do they do that at the French Open?

Every day in golf is wildly different. At Bel Air, pilot Howard Hughes, a member, had a date with Katharine Hepburn, who lived in a house with some other starlets on the par 5 eighth hole. Hughes landed his plane on the fairway, she hopped in, and off they went.

Try *that* on a tennis court.

Best Worst Course Ever

Golf is like sex. Even when it's bad, it's still pretty good. Take the little par 3 I play in Florence, Italy, a place where my wife and I try to live for a month or so every fall because...well, why wouldn't you?

Florence does art, wine, and music angelically. But Florence does golf the way pianos do scuba. There is only one public course in the whole city, a shaggy par 3 that could use a shave and a clean shirt. The first time I went, the taxi dropped me in an empty parking lot. I walked into the pro shop, bought a ticket for nine holes, and asked the pro behind the register where his towels were. I collect the golf towel from every course I play, even the rotten ones.

"Che?"

"Asciugamano da golf," I said. "Golf towel."

"Ahhh!" he said.

He went to the back room and came out with three sheets of Bounty paper towels. "Eccoli!" he said proudly.

The course looked like it hadn't been maintained much since Michelangelo played. Brown greens, sand-free bunkers, fairways that were a nice match for Florence's ancient cobblestone streets. I was the only one on the course and I could see why.

But as I finished, I noticed the empty parking lot was suddenly packed with Mercedes, Ferraris, even a couple Maseratis. On the shady dining porch outside the pro shop, there were a couple dozen slick businessmen in Canali suits and pocket flourishes, smoking hand-rolled cigarettes and waiting for...*what?*

Curious, I sat down next to a Pavarotti-looking dude and gave him a curious look.

"Aspettiamo," he said. *We wait.*

I waited. Nothing.

"Pazienza," he said.

I waited some more.

Then, suddenly, two large-bosomed women with caterpillar eyebrows came out from the back with steaming plates of fresh rigatoni with wild boar ragù, trays of delicate veal piccata, tiramisu to make you weep, all for 10 euros, with a glass of chianti *incluso*. My taste buds sang an aria.

I found myself playing that awful par 3 a lot that fall, taking one off my handicap and adding two to my waist size. You gotta go there someday.

Bring your own golf towel.

Hackers' Heaven

The famous poker player Dewey Tomko once won a golf course in a game of Texas Hold'em. I'd love to win a golf course in a poker game because then I could give it to my son Jake. This is because Jake wants to have his own course someday and, in fact, has already written out the house rules:

1. First hole doesn't count. Nobody has time to warm up and it's no fun, anyway. Unless you *like* your score on the first hole, then you can throw out another hole along the way. Up to you.

2. All trees are on wheels.

3. Oh, and every tree is the Brazilian Deciduous Baobab, which is *exactly* 90 percent air.

4. Until they invent the slice vaccine, every hole is a dogleg right.

5. All tee boxes are blue, so feel free to tell friends you "played the blues," even if the particular set of blues you played are only a few yards longer than the Kroger vegetable aisle.

6. There shall be a box of breakable things on every tee box in case you hit a drive that makes you angry. These items will include old lamps, ancient Chinese vases, and Nickelback records.

7. There's no need to buy one of those indecipherable green-reading books. Every green is a bowl.

8. The first 100 yards of every fairway is green-painted concrete, so if you top one, you still get a nice run out.

9. No lost balls allowed. If your child was lost, would you consider her gone? No, you'd know she was out there somewhere, you just haven't found her yet. It's the same with golf balls. They're not lost, they're just momentarily misplaced somewhere right around here. Is it fair to charge yourself two strokes for a ball you know is sitting *right around here*? No, it is not. So just drop it in the vicinity and add a slight foot foozle for your trouble.

10. Break 100 or your money back.

11. Each player shall get three floating mulligans per side and one traveler mulligan. Also one My Foot Slipped and one You Were Talking on My Backswing. Also one I Don't Goddamn Care, Frank, I'm Taking Another Goddamn One.

12. Additionally, each player will get one Phone a Friend, in which one of our 27 friendly golf pros roving the course in golf carts will come hit your shot for you.

13. Fifteen-inch holes.

14. You might never notice, but there are 50-foot-high, clear Plexiglas walls along the entire boundary of the golf course. A little hard for birds, but great for birdies.

15. Bunkers are merely brown-painted grass. Kind of like Cleveland Browns games.

16. Each cart comes with an extendable eight-foot putter, so almost everything's inside the leather.

17. The bartender with the icy beer keg in the back of your cart is there to serve you, free of charge, and occasionally toss you another ball when nobody's looking.

18. Water hazards in showers only.

19. Throwing allowed.

20. Assume any awkward or difficult lie was caused by a burrowing animal. That's fair as we plan to get one sometime.

21. Tee up anywhere you like. This isn't the damn Masters.

22. When you're done, we use the Harriman Adjusted Potential Index, which takes your score, multiplies it by 66 percent, takes off all chunks, chili dips, and skulls—which

probably weren't your fault anyway—and spits out your actual HAPI score.

23. No bitching.

Although we don't think we'll hear any.

FATHER

I BECAME A FATHER at 27. Kellen came out of the womb looking right at me, eyes wide open, with this peaceful look. Something about this kid's old-soul ways made me realize I had to find peace with my own dad.

He'd stopped drinking seven years before but I just couldn't bring myself to confront him about the mess he'd made inside me. I'd finally played golf with him, but not much. He had a beautiful, slow, Gene Littler reverse-C kind of swing, straight but short. How could someone who made golf seem so ugly have a golf swing so pretty?

Finally, I found neutral ground, a safe place where we could talk— the Masters. He was 70 and he'd never been. I'd never been on a single road trip alone with him. On the two-hour rental-car ride from Atlanta to Augusta, I inhaled deep, put a death grip on the steering wheel, and said it.

"Why were you such a crappy dad?" I asked. "You always coming home drunk from golf. Drunk and mean. And scary. We'd all have to hide. You did that every weekend. You never came to any of my baseball games. You never came to anything." I could feel myself well up. My voice got higher. It was like the eight-year-old me was finally standing up to him. "Why were you like that?"

He turned in his seat toward me and said, "I'm so sorry." He said all he thought about was where his next drink was coming from. Not his wife, not his kids. He apologized for what a lousy dad he'd been, for never being around. "I know. I know I was terrible to you kids and Mom."

"Why, though?" I said. "Why did you let yourself get like that?"

He said he was the son of a small-town doctor who never gave him any attention, so he'd get drunk, get in fights, get thrown in jail, just to get him to notice him. Flunked out of two colleges drinking. He'd had a first wife none of us kids knew about. He married her just before WWII, but when he came home, thinking they'd start a life together and have a family, she refused to come out of her mother's house to even speak to him. They had the marriage annulled without him ever getting to talk to her about it.

He must've said "I'm sorry" 20 times on that single car ride and I finally forgave him, and in the forgiving, I suddenly felt so incredibly light, the seat belt was the only thing keeping me from floating away.

That day freed me. Freed me from my bitterness toward him, freed me from blaming my own problems on him, freed me to live my life and concentrate on my own kids.

Like any sane dad, I gave them golf.

My Dad Is Missing

It may have been the most notebook-dropping press conference in golf history.

In 2015, Billy Hurley III, a PGA Tour pro, walked to the mic on the Tuesday of the Quicken Loans National tournament in Virginia and stared out at the assembled reporters. Suddenly, his face caved in, he flushed red and dissolved into tears.

"My dad is missing," he said.

His father, a cop, was suddenly just…gone. He was not a drinker and had no history of mental illness. His marriage seemed as normal as a Norman Rockwell painting. But nine days before, he'd disappeared with some cash, some clothes, and his truck, and without leaving even a note. This presser was all his son could think to do.

"There were two things my dad could do on a computer," Hurley remembers now. "Check his email and check my scores. He always knew what I'd shot that day." So Hurley convinced his mom and his siblings to let him stand up at the tournament press conference and send their father a message.

He said that day, "I'm just hoping that maybe he goes to PGATour.com to check my tee time or check my score and sees this and understands that, Dad, we love you and we want you to come home."

The irony was that his father had worked at this same Robert Trent Jones Golf Club as a cop protecting Presidents Cup players like Fred Couples and Ernie Els. Plus, this was the Tour's annual celebration of the military, and Billy Hurley, a graduate of the US Naval Academy, remains the only graduate of any military academy to earn a Tour card, serving for five years as a combat electronics officer in the Persian Gulf, where he played exactly zero golf.

Not that he didn't try. He brought a couple clubs and a giant bag of old balls aboard the USS *Chung-Hoon*, only to find out the navy only allows its sailors to hit water-soluble balls off its flight decks.

And yet when he got out of the navy, Hurley had this crazy idea to try pro golf, at 27, having played less golf than a submarine commander.

His dad was all for it. He'd been a collegiate golfer himself and a club pro, too. Plus, he'd taught his son the game, but *his* way. "Feelings are not reality," his dad told Billy a hundred times.

"Always stay level. Don't play with emotion. Don't get excited over a birdie and don't get mad over a double bogey."

Which is exactly how Will Hurley Jr. lived his own life. "My dad was very black-and-white," Billy remembers. "He was very stoic. He didn't show his emotions. Actually, I think that was part of his demise."

As Billy started playing golf again—hitting mostly military courses because he could play them for free—he found out just the opposite. "I figured out you *have* to experience the elation of a birdie and the disappointment of a double bogey," he says. "Because feelings *are* real. You have to deal with those feelings— clear them—and then move on to the next hole. Because when you don't let them out, they come out later and you have no idea why or where it's from, because it's mixed up with 10 or 20 other emotions you bottled up with it."

Therapy—and a flawless golf swing that didn't rust from high school—helped him work his way up through the game until he earned his Tour card in 2011. Cut to that stunning press conference four years later. Three days after it, a woman in the public library in Texarkana, Texas, was reading a piece about Hurley's dad when she looked up and saw him, using the computer.

She called the police. But Mr. Hurley wasn't answering questions. "I haven't broken any laws," he told them. "I'm traveling." They had no choice but to let him go.

Sixteen days later, he killed himself with a shotgun. Whatever he was feeling that day, he kept it inside. He left no note.

"I got a voice mail," Billy remembers. "It was from the sheriff. He said, 'Billy, I'm here with your mom. She's fine. But I need you to call me right away.' That's when I knew he was gone."

The next nine months were a lot of moonless nights and

sunless days. He lost his Tour card. He lost his desire. "It was just like, 'Golf sucks. Life sucks,'" Hurley remembers. "I had a very serious conversation about quitting with my wife." But Heather told him to give it more time.

Good thing. Because not long after that talk, he started playing better. By the time he got to the Quickens again, he was playing the best golf of his life. Almost one year to the day after his distraught Quicken Loans press conference, he was having a happy Quicken Loans tournament, as the leader.

"That whole week I just had this overwhelming sense of peace," he said. He was no longer his father's son. He was just himself. He was playing with Ernie Els, who was one shot behind him, the same Ernie Els his father had guarded.

"I remember we had some cops walking with us because we were the final group," Hurley recalls. "We were going from 9 to 10 and I was thinking, 'Wow, my dad did this exact same thing these cops are doing.' And that felt sad, thinking about my dad and how I wished he were there, walking with me. But I acknowledged that emotion and I let it go. I dealt with it and then went on to thinking about hitting the next shot."

Each shot was nearly perfect. A chip-in on 15 and a 30-foot bomb on 16 gave Hurley a lead that even Els couldn't catch. After Hurley putted out on 18, Els came up, hugged him, and said, "Your dad would be so proud of you."

Billy Hurley III still grieves his father. But in a strange way, he's a better man now. "It forced me into growth I didn't want. I had to learn so much. I had to learn about myself. I had to learn that you have to use what works for you, not anybody else. I'm just me. I'm not my dad. I can't hit shots like Tiger Woods. I have to hit shots like Billy Hurley, and sometimes that's good enough."

Barefoot in the Park

My middle child, Jake, is a born rebel. For the high school talent show, he set three kinds of dog food in bowls in front of a dog for a taste test. The dog salivated. He took a big spoonful from the first bowl and...ate it himself. The audience groaned. The dog turned his head curiously at him. He declared the second bowl the best. At a Head Boy presentation, he wore a red sequined gown and heels. At the golf team tryouts his freshman year at Denver's City Park Golf Course, he made a hole in one, barefoot.

But here's the thing. That's only the third-most-famous barefoot thing to ever happen at City Park.

The first was done by City Park's legendary head pro, Tom Woodard, when he was in college. The best player on the University of Colorado golf team—and the only Black #1 in NCAA Division I golf—he was driving to Fort Collins to play in the quarterfinals of the 1963 state amateur match play championship when he realized he'd forgotten his golf shoes.

"I had street shoes on," remembers Woodard, now elegantly gray-haired. "That wasn't going to work. I didn't have any money. I didn't have a credit card. I didn't know what I was going to do."

But then Woodard remembered a Hawaiian priest named Father Monaghan who famously played City Park nearly every day in bare feet and bare chest. "I decided, 'Well, I'll play barefoot.'"

When Woodard arrived unshod at the first tee, his opponent looked at him like he'd just dropped in from the moon. "Playing barefoot isn't as hard as you might think," Woodard says. "You just can't swing as hard as you usually do, but I never swung hard anyway."

In golf, swinging easier will almost always make the ball go straighter, which means you'll be in a lot more fairways, which will feel good on your tootsies. "In fact," Woodard says, "Sometimes I'll give lessons and have people take off their shoes and socks, just for that purpose."

(You don't have to tell former Chicago Bears QB Jim McMahon. He *only* plays barefoot, no matter where he is, even Arizona. Having had more than one broken ankle, he says his feet and shoes just don't get along. "Besides," McMahon likes to say. "Golf is about balance, right? When you're barefoot, you can feel your balance better.")

You can guess what happened to Woodard that day. He kept his feet on the soft stuff and drilled his opponent 3 and 2. It was huge news in the state and then spread like fungus. Of course, since Woodard is Black, it got twisted. Somehow people thought Woodard couldn't afford golf shoes.

"I *had* golf shoes," Woodard insists. "I just forgot them. But the story suddenly became I was this poor kid who didn't have shoes." People even sent him shoes, thinking he was a charity case.

The racism didn't stop during Woodard's eight seasons on the PGA Tour. "They weren't used to seeing a Black player on Tour," he remembers. "More than a few times I'd get to the first tee at the start of a tournament and one of the officials would say, 'OK, who are you caddying for?'"

Woodard would just bend his knee, grab the toe of his shoe, and show the guy his spikes.

"Player," he'd say.

You can say that again.

The Woman Who Won the Masters

OK, so you think you know everything there is to know about the Masters? Let's see how you do on my Mini Masters Quiz...

Q: Who are the only two pro golfers ever invited to join Augusta National?

A: ˙snɐlʞɔıN ʞɔɐſ puɐ ɹǝɯlɐԀ plouɹ∀

Q: How many times did Bobby Jones break par at the Masters?

A: ˙oɹǝZ

Q: There are 80,000 kinds of plants on Augusta National. How many palm trees?

A: ˙ʎɹots ɐ sǝıl uıǝɹǝɥʇ puɐ ··· ǝuO

Few people know there even is a palm tree at Augusta—it's hidden way right of and behind the fourth green. One of those people is Paul Tesori, the longtime caddy of Webb Simpson, and Vijay Singh before that. In 2012, Tesori and his wife of four months, Michelle, were making their Sunday drive from Florida to Augusta for her first-ever Masters when he offered a wager.

"Honey," he said. "There's only one palm tree on the whole course. If you can find it, I'll buy you that ring you've been wanting." That was some offer, since that wedding band—the one she wanted to go with her engagement ring—was a cool $10,000. Tesori didn't have anything close to $10,000, which tells you how sure he was she'd never find the palm tree.

Two days later, Michelle was in a crowd of 3,000 following Simpson, Rickie Fowler, Jason Day, and Bubba Watson. (Day dropped out with a sore wrist on the third.) On the fourth, Tesori told the boys about the bet.

Watson's head spun toward Tesori, and he suddenly started talking like he'd swallowed a loudspeaker.

"WAIT! ARE YOU SAYING IF MICHELLE SEES THAT PALM TREE OVER THERE," Watson yelled, pointing toward the palm, "THAT YOU'LL BUY HER A $10,000 RING?"

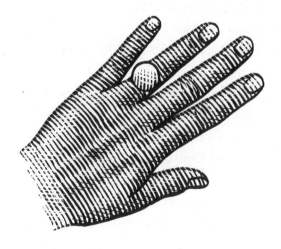

"Shut up, Bubba!" Tesori pleaded. "Michelle is right over there!"

Watson whispered to Tesori: "Pay me $100 and I'll shut up."

"No, just shut up!" Tesori whispered back.

"OK, now it's $200," Watson whispered.

"No!"

"THAT ONE PALM TREE?" Watson yelled again. "RIGHT OVER THERE IN THE CORNER? IF MICHELLE FINDS THAT, IT'S GONNA COST YOU TEN GRAND?"

Tesori shushed him again, but it was too late. He looked over to see Michelle pointing at the palm tree and throwing her arms up in the touchdown signal. Tesori looked like he'd just eaten a bad clam. He glared at Watson.

"All you had to do is pay me the hundred," Watson laughed.

On the fifth hole, Fowler started feeling bad for the caddy. After all, $10,000 is a little steep for guys who eat at Sonic. "Tell you what," Fowler said. "Let's make a deal. If any one of us wins this week, *we'll* buy Michelle the ring."

"Love that idea!" Watson said.

Simpson hated that idea.

"If I win, Paul is gonna get $150,000," Simpson reasoned. "He can buy his own ring."

They decided that was fair enough. But what were the odds one of them would bail Tesori out? None of the three had ever won the Masters before. In fact, none of them had ever won a major before. Tesori kept looking over at Michelle, who kept laughing and grinning.

By Sunday afternoon, Fowler had finished 27th and Simpson 44th, but Bubba was in the hunt. Paul and Michelle were driving home, listening to the tourney on SiriusXM radio and doing a little dreaming. "Can you imagine?" Michelle howled. "If Bubba really *did* win?"

You know what happened next. Watson hit the craziest left-handed hook gap wedge in history out of a forest to save a preposterous par in the playoff and oust Louis Oosthuizen and win the Masters.

Watson cried (Watson always cries), donned the green jacket, and was eating the winner's dinner afterward with his caddy, Fowler, and a few others when something snapped him straight up in his chair.

"Whoa!" he said. "Guys! Do you have any idea what this means?"

Of course, his buddies said. *This changes your life. You're a Masters champ forever—*

"No!" he said. "I gotta buy Michelle that ring!"

He bought it, too, though the jeweler thought the whole thing was so funny he took 25 percent off.

But that's not the end of the story. Turns out there was some magic in that ring. Not only did Watson win that Masters, Fowler won at Quail Hollow a month later. The month after that, Simpson won the US Open at the Olympic Club. And Jason Day, who'd dropped out the hole before? He went into a winless slump that lasted two years. "Some crazy karma in that ring," Tesori says.

Crazier still: When's the last time you heard of one guy giving another guy's wife a wedding ring and nobody getting divorced over it?

Congratulations. I Hate You.

In her very first day playing golf, on her very first course, on the fifth hole she'd ever played, using her fiancé's 8 iron, 32-year-old Elisabeth Kanter made a hole in one.

Her fiancé, filmmaker Jade Deyoe, wasn't even looking. He was opening a beer in the golf cart.

"Hey, babe?" she said.

"Mmmmh?" he said, gulping.

"I think it went in."

"What?"

"The grass ate my ball."

"Wait," her fiancé said, choking on his swallow. "What?"

"My ball. I think it fell in the hole."

Her fiancé suddenly jumped out of the cart like there was a rattler in it. "What? You just made a hole in one?"

"Yeah," she said, surprised at the way he was holding his haircut. Kanter, having never played golf before, thought it was nice to make a hole in one, but nothing special. "I figured Tiger Woods made one or two every round," she says.

She was actually even a little bugged. They'd had a tiff that morning about the wedding invitations. She wanted her name to read "Dr. Elisabeth Kanter" because she'd earned a doctorate in philosophy. Deyoe didn't like the idea. "I was kind of hurt by that," she confessed. "Like, he didn't appreciate what a big achievement that was for me. But I make a hole in one and he loses his mind."

And he did. Beer was flying everywhere as he ran around, jumping and hugging her. They sped toward the hole and found her TaylorMade (well, *his* TaylorMade) sitting in the hole.

The fiancé yelled to nobody, "She just made a hole in one!" The group behind started whooping. Jade insisted they drive in and tell the pro, which they did, and he gave her a signed certificate.

On this date, July 26, 2021, the grass ate Elisabeth Kanter's ball.

But when she called her dad, who isn't a golfer, he seemed unimpressed.

Kanter: Hey, I went out the other day and golfed for my first time ever, and I got a hole in one.

Dad: Is that good?

Kanter: Well, that's what they're telling me.

Dad: No sh*t? Anything else?

Then she called a golfing friend to get her reaction. "She does a par game, I think," Kanter says.

Me: A par game?
Kanter: You know. She hits it in par.
Me: Got it.

But the friend wasn't in. And that's when Kanter made her big mistake. She posted it on Reddit. She decorated the ball with the words *Hole in One* in pink, took a picture of it, and posted it with the caption "First day of golf—First hole in one. 90 yards. Time to retire."

Uh-oh.

"This post is gonna piss off a lot of people," was the first comment.

"This is bullshit," was the second.

"Congrats. I hate you, but congrats." There was also:

- "Way to go!...Now go to Hell."
- "I've been golfing for 25 years. I golf a lot. I golf with good golfers. I've never even witnessed a 1."
- "Congratulations...excuse me while I go scream at the clouds."

A few people said since it wasn't 100 yards, it wasn't legit. But the best exchange was this one:

Commenter: "This is a lie."
Kanter: "I have a certificate, sir."

Anyway, this is about when Kanter finally realized a hole in one is a rather large thing. And a hole in one in your first hour of your first day playing golf is a thing that's just going to annoy the ever-loving bejesus out of the rest of us.

She wasn't trying to upset people. She only went in the first place because her fiancé's mom backed out and he talked her into it with promises of letting her drive the cart and bringing a cooler full of beers. They went to the Welk Resorts' par 3 course in Escondido, California. On the fateful hole, Jade wanted her to hit a 5 iron, but "I've played a TON of video golf," Kanter says, "and even I knew that was too much. So I took the 8."

Ninety yards, 8 iron. Seems right.

She stood over the ball, having no idea what she was doing since nobody had told her the first thing about how to play. "He just gave me the club and said, figure it out...so that's what I was doing. I don't even know how to hold it."

Jade said to write TaylorMade and tell them, and she did, and they sent her a bag tag commemorating the event. Only one problem: Kanter doesn't have a bag...because Kanter doesn't have clubs.

Maybe you should call it quits while you're ahead?

"Yeah, this game is just too damn easy," she says, laughing. "Nah, it's really fun and relaxing and I get to be with Jade. So I think I'll stick with it."

When the ace happened, she was two weeks away from her wedding. She was taking suggestions on ways to incorporate the ace in the ceremony. I said that after the kiss, the crowd should make a silver tunnel of 8 irons the couple could walk under. She said she'd think about it.

Whatever you do, don't post it.

"He's Not a Real Person"

My sons, my nephews, my brother, my friends, everybody wants to know about Tiger Woods, the most thrilling player golf has ever known. The problem is, there's no way to describe how astonishing Tiger is. The only way is to take you there...

Indianapolis, 1995—I was traveling with Tiger and his dad, Earl. Tiger was still in college. We were in Indy and Tiger was putting on a free clinic at a traditionally Black golf course, which he does a lot. His dad set a beer cooler out on the range at exactly 96 yards. Then he set 10 balls in front of Tiger, who proceeded to knock two of the ten into the cooler. The crowd looked at each other like he was David Copperfield.

I was used to seeing the kid doing paranormal things with a club and a ball. One day at the Stanford driving range, he had his driver in his hand and he had me stand 90 degrees from him and roll golf balls at him, which he'd crush long and straight, every time. You read that right. Tiger crushed moving golf balls, bouncing along the grass, with a driver, every single time.

Presidents Cup, 2009—We're not the only ones blown away by Tiger Woods. Even his rivals get knocked over backward. This was on Saturday afternoon foursomes. Back in the team room, the US caddies and players, including Phil Mickelson, were watching the telecast anxiously. The match was tied and the Americans really needed a point. Woods had 235 yards to the hole. He drew a 3 iron and absolutely strafed the pin and he knew it. Not only did he give the club a full twirl but he held it out with his left hand like a Musketeer holding the sword that had just beheaded the evil cardinal. In the team room, Mickelson jumped off the couch, over the coffee table, landed, spun back, and hollered to the rest of the team, "Boys, doesn't it feel great to be on the right side of *that sh*t* for a change?"

Sherwood, California, 2001—Vijay Singh had a six-shot lead over Tiger on the ninth hole Sunday. He was looking at four feet for birdie while Tiger had 70 feet just to save par. "So," remembers Singh's caddy that day, Paul Tesori. "It's gonna be a two-shot swing, at least, and we're probably going to make the turn with an eight-shot lead. But then Tiger *makes* his seventy-footer. He goes berserk, like he just won a major. And I'm thinking, 'C'mon dude, you're still going to be seven down after this hole.'" Except Singh then three-putted the bunny and the lead was cut to five. Then Tiger birdied 10, eagled 11, birdied 12, birdied 13, and shot 29 on the back. Singh got sucked into the vortex of the Tiger tornado and lost to him by two. "I hate that damn story," Tesori says.

San Martin, California, 2013—It was Thursday just before Max Homa's first-ever Tour round and who did he find hitting balls next to him but *the* Tiger Woods. "He had a guy out on the range shagging him with a baseball glove," Homa remembers. "He was hitting 5 woods. It was the most jaw-dropping thing I ever saw. The guy wasn't even having to move his feet. Every single one went right into the guy's glove. Then he put the 5 wood down and took out a 3 wood. The guy backed up. Same thing. It was the most awesome thing I've ever seen. He's not a real person."

Potomac, Maryland, 2018—When it comes to galleries, Tiger Woods's crowd is the Third Infantry and the rest of golf is two Boy Scouts and a wagon. People run, scream, climb on each other. Choppers hover, photogs jostle, camera crews wrestle. Fans try to sneak under ropes, climb trees, ride shoulders. It's madness. "The first time I played with him was the most nervous

I've ever been in my life," says Tour regular Joel Dahmen. "Walking off the first tee, I looked at the enormous gallery and said, 'So this is your world?' And he goes, 'This ain't nothing.' He was super nice, told funny stories. He even told me he was always going to mark even if he was right next to the cup so I could finish the hole without a stampede of people running to the next hole. Amazing."

Glen Abbey, Canada, 2000—Afterward, even Tiger Woods's caddy, Stevie Williams, had to go back to the spot, just to make sure he hadn't dreamed it. On the 72nd hole of the Canadian Open, a par 5, Woods needed a birdie to win. But he was in a pickle—in a bunker, wet sand, 218 yards from the green, blocked from going for the green by bushes, an oak tree, a lake, and common sense. Just to add to the trouble, the pin was tucked far right, against the lake. Everybody was waiting for Tiger to lay it out left. Every golfer who's ever lived lays that shot out left. Everybody but Tiger that is, who struck the world's most perfect 6 iron—over the fans, the bushes, the tree, the lake, and the pin. It sucked to a stop on the back fringe, setting up an easy two-putt birdie for the win. Williams said it was the most amazing shot he ever saw his boss hit.

Afterward, though, Earl saw his son and mumbled, "Well, you didn't hit the green, so it wasn't *that* great."

She's Got This

When Joe Bockerstette's wife was about to deliver their second baby, he had dreams. He was going to coach his daughter up. He was going to be in the stands for her every game, meet, and match. He was going to be her doubles partner.

But when little ginger-haired Amy was born, he knew right away this daughter was going to be different. Amy had Down syndrome. He loved her, but it took him a while to get a grip on what he'd lost.

"You grieve," Joe says. "I realized right away I wasn't gonna have the child I thought I was going to have. I was thinking, 'I'll never watch her play sports.'" Joe pauses. "Well, how silly does that sound now?"

Very.

Spin the clock ahead 19 years—to January 30, 2019, the Waste Management Phoenix Open. As part of a PGA Tour outreach deal, Amy was invited to take a swing at the famous 16th hole par 3 at TPC Scottsdale. That's the hole where 20,000 people yell, chug, and dance *while* pros hit their shots. She'd meet US Open champ Gary Woodland and longtime Tour star Matt Kuchar on the tee box.

"Would you like to hit a shot?" Woodland asked her when they met.

"Yes!" she said.

Nobody expected much. It was the usual thing we do with disabled athletes. Anything she did in front of the 5,000 gathered there—even if she dribbled it off the tee—was going to be greeted like she'd climbed K2. There'd be a lot of "Aww, way to go!"s and "Well, bless your heart!"s. But they didn't know Amy.

Were you nervous?

"No!" she says.

Why the hell not? I've had to hit that shot at 16 twice and I was as nervous as a late-November turkey. The first time, I was so nervous I snap-hooked my 9 iron into the stands. *Clatter, rattle, rolling laughter.* The second time, I barely got it onto the far right edge of the green. I came off the tee dripping with relief.

"My God, that was terrifying," I said to the guy next to me.

"What, this?" the guy said. "Nah."

Turned out to be Tim Tebow. Then he stepped up and hit it to three feet and won the contest.

Amy is like Tebow. She never gets nervous. Amy completely focuses on one shot at a time. Not the one before and not the one after. "She doesn't know whether she got a 3 or a 5 or a 9 on a hole," says Joe, her coach, caddy, and gopher. "For us, it's just the very next shot." Amy isn't trying to make birdies or pars or break 100. She just wants to hit this next shot well. And have fun.

The shot that day was 117 yards. Joe gave her the hybrid 6. Amy reared back and made the same nearly flawless swing she makes every time—good balance, finish with the right shoulder pointing at the target, posing. It rocketed off the club face. The mouths on Woodland and Kuchar fell open in tandem. It flew high and sweet, but a little right and into the bunker.

The crowd went crazy. TV cameras zoomed in on Amy's happy grin. She was looking up at the crowd and waving. Jubilant, the sixsome of Amy, Woodland, and Kuchar and their three caddies walked toward the green. Fans were yelling for her. "They love me!" Amy said to Woodland. "Awesome!"

But her lie in the bunker was not so lovable. The lip in front was taller than Amy. Woodland asked her, "Do you want to hit out?" but in a tone that said, *Let me go get that out of there because that's a very hard shot.*

But Amy replied, "Yes, I do. I got this."

Woodland and Kuchar threw their heads back. Who knew she'd have swagger?

Amy climbed down into the bunker and hit the most

beautiful little escape to within 15 feet of the hole. The crowd went double crazy.

Nobody had to ask her if she wanted to putt it. "Why don't you go ahead and make this?" Woodland said.

"Yeah, I got this," she said again.

She poured it right in the center, perfect speed, par. The crowd went triple nuts. Woodland hugged her and yelled, "You are so awesome!" Amy waved some more and blew the spectators kisses.

That up-and-down goes down as one of the most up moments in Down history. "You're amazing," Kuchar said.

Well, Joe has known that her whole life. She may be intellectually disabled, but she's not athletically disabled. She's got a beautiful golf game and "she's a gamer. The more it matters to her, the more you can bet on her."

Amy Bockerstette, now in her early twenties, is arguably the most famous athlete with Down syndrome in America. She was the first athlete with an intellectual disability to play in the Arizona high school golf tournament. Yeah, you read that right. Amy Bockerstette, who has Down syndrome, played in the actual Arizona high school golf tournament.

Were you scared? I asked her.

"No!" she says. "I was happy!"

She finished 77th out of 90.

Then she became the first athlete with an intellectual disability to ever receive a college athletic scholarship—to Paradise Valley Community College in Phoenix. This was no gift, no publicity gimmick. She was on the team based on her ability to get the ball in the hole, not on her ability to make people feel charitable. She worked her way up the roster to the fourth spot. In one tourney, she finished sixth out of 25.

In 2021, Amy became the first athlete with Down syndrome to play in a national collegiate athletic championship when Paradise Valley went to Florida to compete in the NJCAAs.

Were you nervous?

"No!" she says. "I played with my new friends!"

I'm going to stop asking.

When my daughter, Rae, was 12, I got to coach her school basketball team and I loved it. Joe Bockerstette grieved how he'd never get to do that for Amy. Now he does 100 times the coaching, caddying, and gophering than he ever got to do for his first daughter.

"This whole thing turned out better than my wildest imagination," he says, half-exhausted and half-delighted.

So far 53 million people have seen the video of Amy's Amazing Par at the TPC. No day goes by that Amy doesn't get recognized. And whether they're leaning out of car windows or turning the wrong way on an escalator, they all say the same thing: "You got this!"

Oh, definitely.

GAMBLER

*WHEN I WAS 30, I found the worst course in America, which turned out to be Ponkapoag Golf Course, outside Boston, a course that would have to undergo a federal urban renewal to be considered a dump. I had so much fun there among the inmates at Ponky, I never wanted to leave. They'd play sevensomes. They'd hit each other's balls backward. They'd putt for dollars by car headlight. I wound up writing a comic golf novel out of it—*Missing Links—*and it's still going strong.*

Which is why I was delighted to find a group of idiots in Colorado who were just as sick about golf as the Ponkies. Everything you could think of was allowed: complimentary presses, in-flight presses, and f*ck-you presses, and that was just on the first tee.

"The Usuals" I called them, and they included Sunshine, Simon the Likable, and the ringleader, Lenny (Two Down) O'Connor, the World's Most Avid Golf Gambler, whose hair went straight up and whose drives went straight down and whose blood type was espresso. Two Down would double or nothing his mother in church bingo.

One day, Two Down deemed that the seventh hole would hereafter be known as the Chuckwagon. The team that lost that hole had to buy the grub at the snack shack behind the green. That was fine until one day we got to the seventh tee and saw a giant buffet table waiting, with a white tablecloth, a candelabra, and a chef, complete with giant white hat, carving up prime rib. That's when Two Down hollered, "What's for lunch, Cookie?"

We Usuals traveled all over the country, beating each other out of the *same $20 bill, then losing it in dice afterward, then winning it back the next morning on whether the waitress's first name started with a vowel. We'd give each other constant grief, laugh until our stomachs hurt, and never give an inch, all of which is the way guys say they love each other.*

We are still close today, proving that some links never go missing at all.

$100,000 per Foot

When Christian Sanchez left his $35,000-a-year job as a golf instructor and moved to Las Vegas, he thought maybe life would get a "tad" more exciting.

Wrong.

His life suddenly turned into a high-wire triple backflip with no net.

It all started in 2009, when Sanchez was trying and failing to make a living on the Vegas mini tour and filling in the holes in his checkbook by teaching anybody who came along. That's when he met Daniel Negreanu.

Negreanu is one of the world's biggest poker stars. He has six World Series of Poker bracelets and was named the Poker Player of the Decade in 2014. If Negreanu sits down at your table, this is your cue to get up and leave.

But when he took up golf, a whole mess of his money started flowing the wrong way. In the world of huge-stakes golf gambling, Negreanu was the biggest pigeon in town.

"Those first couple of years cost me $3 million," says Negreanu, who was about a 27 handicap then. "They're on the first tee, hollering out stuff, and I'm writing it down. 'I get 5 a side!' 'I get 8 a side!' I had no idea you could negotiate that. And whaddya know? I lost my ass."

Why would Negreanu bet that much on a sport he'd barely played before? Because "betting on golf is way more thrilling than betting on poker," he insists. "With poker, you can make the right decision and the cards fall and it's out of your control. In golf, if you have a six-footer for $100,000, it's on you, nobody else."

The multimillionaire poker player asked the nearly broke golf instructor to come out to the course the next day and see what he was doing wrong. What Sanchez found was Negreanu getting fleeced like a summer sheep. "This one guy played him as an 8," Sanchez remembers, "and I'd played the same guy, straight up, and he beat me!"

Sanchez put a stop to all that and Negreanu wound up winning big that day. He was hired on the spot to be his teacher, caddy, and occasional non-wagering playing partner—$5,000 a week, plus 5% of anything Negreanu won. That's a minimum $260,000 a year, which Sanchez couldn't have made in a decade of lessons.

Naturally, the first thing Sanchez did was go out and nearly blow the whole gig.

Negreanu wanted Sanchez to be his partner in a $46,000-per-hole match against two poker players, one of whom was scratch. They were playing for more money on one hole than Sanchez made all the previous year. He was so nervous he could barely grip the club. "I went six over for the first seven holes," Sanchez remembers.

"He honestly thought that was it," Negreanu says with a

laugh. "He thought it was his last day on the job." But Negreanu was having a rare good day. Sanchez got his feet under him on the back nine and they wound up winning $100,000.

After that, the pigeon became a shark. "Before I had Christian," Negreanu says, "if I was out there in a big match and my swing fell apart, I was doomed to lose $400,000 or $500,000. But with Christian as my caddy, he can see what's going on—'You're too flat,' 'Your grip is too strong'—and I'm not doomed anymore."

"After that," Sanchez says, "I stopped being nervous."

Not nervous, that is, until The Big Bet.

It started when Negreanu texted Sanchez: "You think I could shoot 80 from the back tees, if I had a year to do it?"

That was a very odd question from a guy who usually shot around 105 from the whites. "It'd be really really hard, but, yeah, maybe," Sanchez replied. "Why?"

"Because Phil Ivey wants to bet me $550,000 I can't do it."

Sanchez thought two things: (a) Ivey was the largest poker star in the world and never made a dumb bet, and (b) 5 percent of over half a million dollars was…well…whatever it was, it was a silo of money for a teaching pro.

Sanchez gulped and wrote: "Yes. I think you can do it."

The rules were these:

- The 80 had to be shot from the back tees at the par 72 TPC Summerlin—nowhere else.
- The round could begin on any hole as long as it was 18 consecutive holes. If it started on 5 and ended on 4, fine.
- If Negreanu was getting close to shooting the 80, he had to immediately call Ivey, who could then hurry out and hurl as much voodoo snakejuice at him as he could.

Of course, this is a patently insane bet. The thing about golf scores is that they get exponentially harder the lower you go. Going from 100 to 90 is three times easier than going from 90 to 80 and that's 10 times easier than going from 80 to 70, which is harder than the Heisenberg uncertainty principle.

"When I made the bet, I didn't know that," Negreanu says. The first time Sanchez took him to the back tees, the poker star shot a swift 116. If it was poker, Negreanu would've folded.

Negreanu spent the next eleven months playing poker and not working on his game. "I came back and it hit me: 'I've got about a month to go to close this thing out and I haven't been playing at all.'"

That's when Camp Christian kicked in. In those last weeks, he worked Negreanu like a rented mule. They'd practice at the range, play 18, have lunch, practice some more, play another 18, squeeze in a spot of dinner, then play nine more. He even had Negreanu spend some time with Tiger Woods's coach at the time, Hank Haney, who gave the banjo-hitting Negreanu a tip for more distance. ("Swing faster.")

It wasn't going to be near enough.

With 10 days to go, the closest they'd come was 86. As Negreanu says, "The distance between 86 and 80 is a mountain."

With less than a week to go, Negreanu was playing yet another in an endless string of fruitless rounds, trying to cut six shots off his lifetime best of 86 in one giant leap. That day, he started his round on 10 and immediately went bogey, bogey, double.

OK, start the round over at 13.

That's when, out of nowhere, Daniel Negreanu got hot. He parred 13 and 14, birdied 15, parred 16, then made another birdie on 17. He was 2 under through five holes. He texted Ivey: *Hey, I've got a chance.*

Negreanu played the next nine holes without setting himself on fire and found himself needing only four bogeys on the last four holes to shoot exactly 80. *Was this really going to happen?*

Ivey showed up, along with about 60 others, to see if the biggest golf bet anybody had ever heard of was going to cash.

That's when Negreanu started to fall apart. On 9—the first of the four holes—he left his approach in the bunker, then left it in there, on his way to a double bogey. Now he needed one par and two bogeys on his last three holes. But those holes were 10, 11, and 12, the same three holes he'd butchered four hours before. Sanchez stared at his shoes. Ivey was in his cart, smiling.

On 10, 420 yards, par 4, Negreanu hit his usual 240-yard drive, his 210-yard 3 wood, and a wedge that left him 20 feet from the hole. The putt he hit broke a foot and a half and buried itself in the hole like a good little ball. There was the par. Still, he needed two bogeys on two very long holes.

On 11, 448 yards, par 4—good drive, decent 3 wood, weak wedge to 60 feet. He hit the putt six feet by and then somehow made the come-backer. One hole to go. One bogey to go.

"I was so nervous," Sanchez remembers. This moment was a life changer. He and his wife wanted to start a family, but they decided they couldn't do that until they'd bought a house. The $27,500 bonus would be enough to put them over the down-payment hump. But if the boss missed, would Sanchez's days be numbered? When your boss loses half a million dollars, doesn't somebody have to pay?

On 12, 442 yards, par 4—drive, 3 wood, then a lousy wedge that wound up 70 feet from the hole. Two-putt or die. This time the first putt skittered six feet past the hole. So here it was: a putt worth $100,000 per foot.

You sure you wanted this much thrill, Daniel?

As usual, he asked Sanchez to read it. "Just lining up that putt," Sanchez remembers, "I was thinking, 'If I misread this, it's on me. He loses $550,000. I was kind of sick to my stomach.'"

His mouth a dust bowl, Sanchez managed to say: "Little uphill, right to left, about a ball out on the right."

Negreanu stepped up to it, barely able to breathe. "I made a stroke I'd never made in my life," he remembers. "I kinda fell down. I think my knee might have hit the ground. Is that even legal?"

However badly it was struck, the ball didn't seem to know. It snuck into the corner of the hole for the world's most lucrative bogey.

The poker player went running around the green, arms in the air, until he found the teaching pro, and they jumped together like a pitcher and catcher winning the World Series.

Just so you know, Christian Sanchez is a friend of the family. He's pals with two of my nephews and often played against them in junior and high school tournaments in Colorado. So it gives me great pleasure to say he and the poker star are not only still a team, he and his wife are, too. With the money, they bought a home in Vegas and their four daughters make for a very full house.

Let's Get Trashy

You say trees purposely jump out in front of your balls? Does every ball you buy tend to be thirsty? In a round of golf, do you generally find yourself in more bunkers than Saddam Hussein?

Buddy, do I have a tournament for you.

It's called the Trashmasters. And every year, the winner is the golfer who has found more disasters than the Red Cross.

In the Trashmasters—a charity tourney held each summer—you cannot get a point until your ball has hit some trash. If you're one of these people who hits the fairway, then the green, and then two-putts for par, you will finish last. But if you're one of these people who hits it off a spruce, then off a rake, and then gags in a 30-footer for net par, you're going to end up proudly donning the coveted puke-yellow Trashmasters winner's jacket.

You don't get trash for just trees and rocks. You get trash for hitting any ball washer, water cooler, fence, tee marker, electric box, yardage plate, or even one of the many tractors purposely parked in the middle of the fairway, as long as you wind up with a net par. It's so damn much fun that it's drawn the likes of actors Robert Wagner and Michael Douglas, Tour stars Chip Beck and

Scott Simpson, and even former vice president Dan Quayle. And it's not just men. What woman doesn't like to get a little trashy once in a while?

It's very odd to wander upon a Trashmasters tournament—they're now held worldwide—and not quite know what you're looking at. After all, how often do you see four golfers purposely trying to hit their approaches into a pond?

The Trashmasters was invented by a ski instructor named Boone Schweitzer. To play in his Boone-doggle, you must swear to do your trashiest. Literally. Before play begins, Schweitzer makes every player stand and raise their right hand as he asks them, "Do you solemnly swear to play the trash, the whole trash, and nothing but the trash, so help you golf?"

They do. Often astonishingly. One year, a 16 handicap named Tom Wenzel came to a simple par 5 and turned it into a kind of Bruce Willis action film. His tee shot skipped off a pond, hit a rock, bounced off a tree limb, and wound up back in the fairway. Amazing, right? Please. Mr. Wenzel was only getting warmed up.

His second shot, a 3 wood, bounced off a cart path, hit a bridge, and bounced into a creek.

He wasn't done yet.

Wrong Way Wenzel then dropped out of the creek and skulled his approach into the bunker. Whereupon he hit, against all logic, a gorgeous bunker shot that rolled happily into the hole.

Whatever Tom Wenzel had just done was so trashy nobody could figure it out. They called in a "Trashmastermind" to decipher what had happened, total up all the glorious trash, and figure in the "bonus trash," not to mention the "multiple trash." Two burnt calculators later, it was announced that Tom Wenzel had just scored 21 points on a single hole, by far the single trashiest hole in Trashmaster history.

Did he win that year's Trashmasters?

Did Elizabeth Taylor own a wedding dress?

Icarus

Fifty-five isn't just the speed limit. It's the limit of how low mankind can go in a single round of golf.

On May 12, 2012, an Aussie touring pro named Rhein (pronounced REE-IN) Gibson shot a 55. This is not a misprint. Playing with two witnesses, Gibson, then 26, recorded a 12-birdie, two-eagle, four-par, bogey-free, 16-under, honest-to-Jesus 55 at the par 71 River Oaks Golf Club in Edmond, Oklahoma.

It's the best round of golf since they invented the game. But then it's only been around since the mid-1400s.

Naturally, I didn't believe it, so I called him.

No way.

"Way," Gibson said. "It's in *The Guinness Book of World Records*."

Take a mulligan on 1?

"Nope."

Ever come close to 55 since?

"Never even sniffed it."

As you might expect, on this momentous day, Gibson was hungover.

"There was a big party the night before," says Gibson, who floats between the PGA Tour and the Korn Ferry. "I had a little headache. Wasn't feeling too flash."

Beware the hungover guy?

"Right. Lowered expectations really help in golf. I made

everything I looked at. Everything went right into the middle of the hole. It was almost Kevin Na–ish (see page 219). Like, I'd look at a putt and *know* I was going to make it."

I told my son about the 55.

"No way," Jake said.

Way.

"Mulligans?"

Nope.

There was a pause on the line. Then he said, "How many mulligans would it take *you* to shoot 55 at that same course?"

That shut me up. I thought about it. I bet him $5 I could do it in less than 100 mulligans. He took the bet, rather quickly.

I asked Mr. 55 his opinion.

"Hoo-man," Gibson said. "I'll take over 100. Way over 100, maybe 150."

Why?

"Because I reached a few of the par 5s in two. You'll never do it. You'd have to knock irons in from the fairway."

Pah! I got on the plane.

At River Oaks—a private club in the suburbs of Oklahoma City—I met my playing partners: Ryan Munson, a scratch who'd played with Gibson that morning, and Ryan's father, Curtis.

How many? I asked Ryan.

"I think you can do it in less than 100 mulligans," he said. "But I would use your mulligans trying to hit it close, rather than on putts."

I was starting to like this Ryan guy.

We set off to the 10th, which is where Gibson started that day, opening with a par. Me, I made a natural birdie. Take that, Jake.

Score so far: Gibson even par; Reilly -1; Mulligans 0.

11th hole (his second)—This is a long, nasty par 5 Gibson eagled by getting pin high in 2 and then chipping in for eagle. "There might not be enough mulligans in the world for you to reach this green," Ryan said.

I was starting to hate this Ryan guy.

Didn't matter. I'd already jumped this hurdle in my mind. Nobody said anything about shooting 55 *exactly* the way Gibson did. The bet was whether I could shoot 55 using less than 100 mulligans. Period. So if that included no eagles and 16 birdies, so be it. (Hey, find your own quest.)

I hit it on in 3 and made the putt for another natural birdie, if you don't count the four very helpful mulligan putts I took.

Gibson -2, Reilly -2, Mulligans 4.

12th hole (his third)—Gibson birdied this. So did I, but this time it took seven mulligans, all putts. OK, maybe this wasn't going all that well.

Gibson -3, Reilly -3, Mulligans 11.

13th hole (his fourth)—Gibson eagled this par 5, too, his second in three holes.

Flashback:

"Just eagled 11 and 13," Gibson texted to one of his gambling opponents playing behind him.

The reply: "Wanker."

Wanker -5, Reilly -4, Mulligans 14.

14th, 15th, and 16th (his fifth, sixth, and seventh)—Gibson's putter was so hot at this point it was close to burning a hole in his bag. He birdied all three with dead-center putts. On one of them, maybe 25 feet, he bragged to Ryan, "I'm gonna make this." He did.

I birdied all three, too, using up a total of only seven measly mulligans. I was playing as good as I can possibly play. I think it's because when I have dozens of mulligans in my back pocket, I swing freely without my two constant companions: self-loathing and abject fear.

Gibson -8, Reilly -7, Mulligans 21.

17th hole (his eighth)—Whenever I get hot, which is rare, I always tell myself: *Stop it! Who do you think you are?* And then I return to my usual cozy crappiness. Whenever Gibson started to think about how hot he was, he chased it out of his mind and replaced it with, *Let's just hit a solid shot here.* "That was my thought all day," he recalls. " 'Let's just hit this one good and solid. Nothing else matters.' "

Good advice alert

Gibson made yet another birdie, this one easier than the last few, and noticed the grass wasn't beneath his feet anymore. If a 180-pound man carrying a bag can float, Rhein Gibson was doing it.

Me, I made birdie, too, and only used two mullies. I wanted to text my son to tell him but feared he'd call me something worse than a wanker.

Gibson -9, Reilly -8, Mulligans 23.

18th (his ninth)—This is a nasty uphill par 4 with an evil green. I hit my approach to 35 feet and then wasted nine freaking mulligans, seven of them on putts. I was about to try an eighth when Ryan *ahem*ed. I looked at him. He gave me the slashed-throat sign.

He was right. I was becoming a mulligan addict. I could get to 100 mulligans on this one hole alone. I gave up and tapped in a six-incher for my first par. That meant I had only one more par to waste.

"I gotta use mulligans trying to get it closer," I told Ryan. "Not trying to make these long putts."

Ryan rolled his eyes. I think he was starting to hate me.

As for Gibson, this is the point in the round when it hit him he was standing on the ninth tee at 9 under par. Has anybody in golf history ever been able to say they were 9 under through eight?

He hit his best drive of the day, then a perfect 8 iron, then a 10-footer that went to bed like a von Trapp child. "When he sunk it, I didn't know what to do," Ryan said. "It was like a no-hitter. You almost don't want to say anything. So I said, 'Damn, you just shot 10 under on one nine! High five!"

Ryan's scorecard read 432–333–323 = 26. That's the sexiest set of numbers I've ever seen.

Gibson -10, Reilly -8, Mulligans 32.

First (his 10th)—Back in 2012, they walked up to the first tee only to find a group of seniors just setting off, most of whose average score was 55 on a single nine. There was a 15-minute wait. Uh-oh. Coolers.

The first hole is the most treacherous on the course—OB on both sides and the wind right in your face. "In college," Gibson recalled, "I'd seen guys hit 7 iron off the tee just to get it in play. It's scary." No wonder he was satisfied to make a simple par, his first par in nine holes, if you can imagine that. I don't know why he was so nervous. I made another natural birdie. BAM.

Gibson -10, Reilly -9, Mulligans 32.

Second (his 11th)—If a par can ever be a disappointment, Gibson's par here that day was. It was his second in a row. Looked like the leprechauns had all gone back to their clovers.

Gibson -10, Reilly -10. Mulligans 33.

Third (his 12th)—Gibson crushed a driver on this par 5, then an iron, and made an up-and-down birdie to right the ship. I stayed with him but it cost me dearly, seven mulligans.

Gibson -11, Reilly -11, Mulligans 40.

Fourth (his 13th)—This is where heaven started breaking loose again for Gibson. It's a long par 3 into the wind but Gibson hit an iron that was so perfect it would've made you weep. There was nowhere else for it to go but in the hole. It disappeared.

Munson and the third player, Eric Fox, just about lost it. "Dude, nobody's gonna believe this if that went in!" Ryan said. But when they got there, the ball was sitting a quarter inch behind the hole. You could've burped it into the cup.

Gibson -12, Reilly -12, Mulligans 47.

Fifth (his 14th)—Something about that near ace made Gibson bulletproof. He hit another perfect putt for yet another birdie. Even if he were to only par out from here, he'd still shoot 58. That's Bizarro World.

This is when Ryan started tweeting it out and texting everybody he knew. "I knew this was history and I wanted people to witness it."

I made a kind of ugly birdie, if there is such a thing, using three mulligans. I noticed Ryan wasn't texting anybody about me.

Gibson -13, Reilly -13, Mulligans 50.

Sixth (his 15th)—Disaster. The sixth is a fairly easy par 5 with a green surrounded on three and a half sides by water. I birdied it, for instance, with only three mulligans (all wedges). But Gibson launched a rainmaker off the tee and immediately said, "Uh-oh. That's gonna be a mud ball."

Now, in our Friday group, there is no such thing as a mud ball. We do not acknowledge a mud ball's right to exist. We let you wipe off mud balls because they are the devil's handiwork and God doesn't want you to play them and besides they fly crazy. But Gibson wasn't in our Friday group. His 4 iron went miles right and probably OB.

Turn in your slippers, Cinderella. Ball's over.

It was so far right, Gibson immediately hit a provisional. But when they got down there, it was just sitting in bounds, happy, with an alley between a grove of trees heading to the green. Gibson saved par.

"That's the other thing about Rhein's round," course owner Andy McCormick says. "He parred the easiest par 5 on the course. He usually birdies it or eagles it. I mean, can you imagine if he had?"

No. No, I can't.

Gibson -13, Reilly -14, Mulligans 52.

Seventh and eighth (his 16th and 17th)—By now, there were 20 golf carts following Icarus. People abandoned their rounds to come see it. Teachers aborted lessons and brought their students. The bartender left his post.

On the long downhill par 3 seventh, Gibson rolled in another birdie putt. On the eighth, he faced a straight downhill double-breaker. If he's ever going to miss a putt, this is it, Ryan thought. The ball went in like it was afraid of sunlight.

As for me, it had all gone so well I was going into the last hole needing only a simple par to shoot 55. There is nothing more satisfying than taking money from your kids.

Gibson -15, Reilly -16, Mulligans 56.

Ninth (his 18th)—Gibson was flying so high, there was very little oxygen and people weren't thinking straight. Ryan was mistakenly texting people that if Gibson birdied this last hole, he'd shoot 56. It was actually 55, a feat unequaled in history. Sure, in 1962, American Homero Blancas shot a 55, but that was on a dink-and-putt nine-hole that he played twice. Guinness only recognizes rounds on courses of 6,500 yards or more and Blancas's round was 1,400 short of that. That was for mortals. This was the stuff of gods.

With all those people around, it was chaos. There were text pings going off twice a minute. A guy Gibson barely knew came up and said, "Hey, Rhein, how you playing?"

"Can you believe that?" Gibson recalls. "Here's this guy trying to ice me!"

Gibson didn't make eye contact. "Ask Ryan."

But now he was nervous. The dreamer had been awakened. On the tree-lined par 4 ninth, he blocked his drive right, his worst of the day. It was so bad it was right of the cluster of trees, leaving him a shot over them of about 145 yards.

Buddy, when it's your day, it's your day.

He hit a 9 iron that came down 20 feet from the hole. He stepped up and hit a putt so pure it would've gone into a shot glass.

Fifty-five.

Cue the craziness, the hugs, the screaming, the hair pulling, the dancing, the exultation, and the relief.

Gibson -16, Reilly -16, Mulligans 57, Delayed Inheritance $5.

The man only had 19 putts in 18 holes. I've never heard of anybody having that few putts. Gandalf couldn't have that few putts.

As the Munsons and I sipped Heinekens and talked about the 55 afterward, who walked in but Ol' 55 himself, Rhein Gibson. He's about 5-11, green-eyed, and humble. I started riddling him with questions. Finally, he said, "I know it's a big achievement, but it's not like I'm going to get a 55 tattoo on my arm."

Oh, I would. I definitely would.

Once you hear about it, you never forget the Fabulous 55. The Japanese seem the most obsessed with it. They've flown him over twice—first class—just to meet him. "The man shot a 55," McCormick said. "I mean, we can have a four-man scramble out here and no team is shooting 55."

Naturally, people think it's a lie. They say to him:

- *Oh nice, how many mulligans?* (Again: none.)
- *It was a cupcake course, right?* (No. The slope at River Oaks is 132 and the rating is 72.)
- *You probably didn't putt everything out, right?* (Yep. Every hole ended with his ball hitting the bottom of the cup.)

Gibson looked across the table at me. "So," he said. "How many mulligans?"

"Fifty-seven," I allowed, a little smugly. "Sixteen birdies, two pars."

Gibson snapped his head around to the two Munsons.

"No way," Gibson said.

"Way," they said in unison.

"That's pretty good," he admitted, though his face couldn't hide a smidge of disappointment.

Maybe that would've been a good time to mention I played from the red tees?

The Topper

Correct me if I'm wrong, but I believe I'm the only person who got screwed out of millions of dollars by a giant company and yet still worships that company.

Q: How can you love a golf company that screwed you out of millions?
A: When it's as good as Topgolf.

Topgolf is this genius idea that lets you hit golf balls at a driving range with friends and actually keep score against each other. Using computer-coded balls linked to your driving bay, you can compete against your buddy by hitting wedges at close targets (2 points) or drivers at distant ones (60). Most points wins.

Why do I say this idea is genius? Because I thought of it first.

It's 1996 and I'm writing my golf novel, *Missing Links*, a fictional story of four buddies who play the worst golf course in America and make a bet to see who can sneak on to play the best one, which happens to be right next door.

In the epilogue, one of the characters, Crowbar, winds up a millionaire by inventing the very idea that would become Topgolf.

Here's Crowbar talking about his idea for the perfect golf range. Look it up if you want, page 272:

I'd set up these giant colored pits out on the range. If you knock it in the little 100-yard hole, the computer gives you 5 points. If you knock it in the 150-yard hole, the computer gives you 10 points. All the way up to the big

300-yard hole way the hell out there that everybody is trying to reach and get 25 points...Each ball would have one of those computer bar code things on it so the computer would know exactly who hit what ball...You could bet your buddy. You could compete against what you did last time. You could have tournaments.

The book is published in 1997. Two years after that, I get an email from a guy I went to high school with: "Hey, I'm working for a golf company in England that could have stolen your idea. It's so similar that it could have come straight out of your book. Remember Crowbar?"

I reread that email five times without blinking. I look into it all, find it to be true, and hire a New York patent attorney, who winds up telling me it's hopeless.

"Why?" I argue, standing on the couch in his office. "I invented this whole thing! They didn't start making them until the book was out there!"

"Yes, all true," he says, adjusting his glasses, "but you didn't patent the machinery that makes the idea real. That's where the invention is. They made it happen."

One by one, Topgolfs start going up all over the world. Each one of them squirting lemon juice in my eye. It takes me years to get over it, until one day, I go to one in Las Vegas with the golfer Matt Kuchar. It's all so beautifully lit, with waitresses walking around bringing you cold Guinness and chili cheese fries, and golf balls rolling out and teeing themselves up. My god, you don't even have to bend over. If it hadn't been stolen from me, I'd have said Topgolf was the greatest golf invention since the remote- control pull cart.

As I write this, there are now more than fifty Crowbar Inventions, as I call them, peopling the earth, each one more wonderful than the last. In 2021, Callaway bought Topgolf for $2 billion.

Ouch.

I finally spoke to some guy in Topgolf's corporate office in Dallas who would neither confirm nor deny that they'd gotten the idea from my book, but did give me a lifetime membership. Then I found out anybody can buy a lifetime membership to Topgolf for the whopping price of $5.

Teach them to mess with me.

The Day Two Died

In golf, there are more ways to take each other's money than there are dimples at the TaylorMade factory. This truth was taught to me in my 30s by no less than Two Down O'Connor, the World's Most Avid Golf Gambler.

Two Down lives to play golf and gamble and never shall the two be parted. He would no sooner play golf without gambling than Snoop Dogg would smoke without inhaling.

In fact, one time, in Scotland, we found that out.

We were playing Pig and Wolf, a very hilarious game that involves switching partners. There's a "wolf" on each hole and he picks his partner based on their tee shot for just that one hole. If, based on those tee shots, he thinks he can beat everybody in the group on his own, then he becomes the "pig." We were with my buddy Geno and Geno's friend from Dallas, a man who turned out to be a very cautious individual. This guy would call his wife before the round started, at the turn, after the round, after the first beer, and on the way to the next B&B. I was thinking this wife better be Sofia Vergara.

The Cautious Man was very good at making calls, but not so good at making pars. On this particular day, he was down the most money when we got to 17, which meant he not only got to be the wolf on 17 but he got to set the stakes for the hole. This was a great advantage because the wolf has the best chance to win.

So we got to the 17th tee, and we all looked at the Cautious Man to hear the stakes. He was down $23. Some men would try to get it all back on the 17th. Some would go for half on the 17th and the rest on the 18th.

What did the Cautious Man say?

"Zero."

I looked at him and blinked.

"What?" I asked.

"Zero," he said flatly. "I set the stakes at zero."

I leaned toward him, as if my ear canal was suddenly blocked.

"I'm not betting anything," he repeated. "No stakes."

In horror, I snapped my neck toward Two Down, wondering how this unheard-of thing would hit the world's most avid golf gambler.

Two Down looked like he'd been stuck in the forehead with a sharp axe. His face went bloodless, his eyes wide as soup bowls. He turned his head in all directions.

"Wait. What?" he said.

"Zero," the Man from Dallas said. "Nothing."

Two Down's power of speech had left him. He looked at me, imploring me with his eyes to fix this.

"Zero?" I asked.

"Yes. I set the stakes at zero. I don't want to bet anything."

"But...but...but," Two Down cried. "You can't DO that!"

"Why not?"

"Because," Two Down moaned, looking at a man who was the living embodiment of everything he didn't believe in, "you just...you just...you have to bet SOMETHING!"

"I am betting something," the Cautious Man said. "I bet zero. Next two holes, the bet is zero."

It was like somebody told Two Down that Coors stopped making beer.

"But...then...," he asked, "why would we even...*play* the last two holes?"

"For fun?" the Man from Dallas said.

Two Down looked at me and then back at the Cautious Man and then at the clouds and then at Geno and then at the grass and then at the Very Cautious Man again. Two looked like he might either explode or expire. I backed up two steps. I thought he might calmly walk over to the guy's bag and break every club over his knee.

His shoulders sank and his head bowed to the ground. Then he turned and walked into the clubhouse. What's the point of fishing a dry river?

FAN

I'VE BEEN COVERING PRO golf since 1979, but I've never seen a generation of young players come along like this one—Jordan Spieth, Rory McIlroy, Collin Morikawa, Justin Thomas, Rickie Fowler. So many. They're smart. They're fit. They're tight. They care about each other. If one of them is about to win, the others hold the private jet so they can all root their buddy on. At a lot of majors, they all pile into one big house together.

You think Hogan and Snead waited around to congratulate the other? You think Greg Norman and Nick Faldo went dutch on a house? Norman came in by submarine and rented a beach mansion with his agent. Faldo would come in by helicopter and rent a house near the practice range with David Leadbetter.

I can honestly say golf has never been in a better place. And it's not just the new players. It's the new courses, the new technology, the new clubmakers.

We've got cool shirts and high-top golf shoes. I mean, Bubba Watson owns a hovercraft golf cart that can go across water. And thanks to social media, we get to see inside their lives. Most of these players—men and women—are funny, open, and honest. Some of them are so good telling their own stories, it's made me wonder: Why do they need golf writers?

Max Talent

Every single person I've covered in pro golf was a better player than me. But I took comfort in knowing that at least I was a better writer than them.

But now, with Max Homa, I'm not so sure.

Homa isn't just a multiple winner on Tour, he's a wildly creative wordsmith. The speed of his club head is surpassed only by the speed of his wit. Sometimes his tweets are so good, I want to toss my MacBook out the window.

For instance, during the '21 Dallas Tour stop, one of his Twitter followers complained that pros like him need to stop whining about the course setup and "just start playing better."

Homa tweeted back:

Playing better is definitely something I strive for. In my defense, however, I'm not even playing in the tourney.

Another troll ripped him for costing him a large bet. Homa:

I'm sorry you suck at gambling.

Once, at the end of a bad day, he wrote:

Didn't play well but was fortunate enough to have a stranger watch me pee into a cup after the round so it's actually been a pretty solid day all-in-all

Homa has this pithy way of summing up the world of Tour life. After a bad performance at a far-flung Tour event, he tweeted from coach of a United flight:

Airplane middle seat: the most consistent missed cut punishment

Here's Homa giving fans a look into the psyche of a touring pro:

> While walking off the 18th tee today, nearing the end of a pretty difficult, breezy day, my caddy said that if golf were easy it wouldn't be fun. It was a deep and philosophical comment. I wanted to punch him

I told Homa he could write for a living. He scoffed. "I have enough trouble playing golf," he said. But he is good enough. For instance, during the 2017 season, Homa hit an ice patch of 15 missed cuts in 17 tries. He wrote:

> Had a few caddies hit me up recently hoping to team up. They heard they usually get weekends off which is apparently a great selling point

Stuff like this started getting Homa hundreds of thousands of followers. Pretty soon, fans started sending him videos of their swings, asking for his critique. A follower named Matt Trustcott sent in his video and added that he was really frustrated and was "prepared to quit the game completely." Homa replied:

> Trust ur gut.

On the swing of Twitter follower Mike Rohde:

> what you lack in confidence you also lack in swing speed

"My best round is probably better than yours," Ryan McPherson wrote.

> apparently not cuz i have no idea who the hell you are.

Pretty soon celebrities started asking to be Maxxed. Milwaukee

Brewers star Christian Yelich sent in a video of him actually whiffing a shot.

> i'm going to tell [Dodgers pitcher Clayton] kershaw the way to strike you out is to just walk up to the plate and put it on a tee

Homa grew up just north of LA. As a kid, he'd play with his dad at Vista Valencia muni and then sit on the wall behind the range while his dad went in for a beer. "I'd watch all these different swings," Homa remembers. "And I'd kind of analyze them. Then my dad would come out and say, 'Don't look at these golf swings. They're awful.' And now I have to see all kinds of bad swings on my feed."

On the other hand, if you want to see pure butter, watch Homa's swing. A sensational ball striker, Homa once went eye to eye with no less than Rory McIlroy at the Wells Fargo and won. He had one of the most emotional triumphs on Tour in years when he beat Tony Finau in a playoff to win the 2021 LA Open at Riviera, a tournament his dad had taken him to every year since he was two.

People started coming out of the digital woodwork. A dude living in Illinois named Armin Abdic started begging Homa on Twitter to play with him. Abdic tweeted:

> Day 1 of tweeting at @maxhoma23 to play a round of golf with me

Homa:

> Day 1 of me saying I'm busy that day

Abdic kept asking. Homa kept finding new ways to turn him down. After Day 4's request, Homa tweeted back:

Wow honestly thank u for the invite but I have so many errands to do that day plus I need to eat like 3 meals. I'm gunna be slammed.

After Day 9:

Dang it's crazy u picked that day of all days because I had already planned to play with a random dude I met from Instagram.

After Day 12:

I checked the weather that day and it looks like there's a 1% chance of rain so I'm gunna have to bail sorry dude.

After Day 20, in which Abdic included a video of his buddy's swing:

Damn that's bad. Let him know if he ever needs some help to reach out cuz I'm pretty free for a while! Except that one day u suggested. I'm busy that day unfortunately

Finally, after Day 25, Homa abdicated. "I was out of comebacks," Homa recalls. "I was dying trying to think of a new one for this guy, so I gave in."

Somebody once asked Homa where all this stuff comes from. "My brain's messed up," he decided. "It's a beautiful disaster." That's the best kind.

Na Problem

Kevin Na has been known for many things, not all of them good.

For a while he was known as the guy who played slower than cold honey tipped out of a jar.

Then he was known as the guy who won a $200,000 car and gave it to his caddy.

Then he was known as the guy whose Korean fiancée's parents picketed outside the gates of a 2014 tournament to protest him breaking up with their daughter. (It's a Korean thing.)

Then he was known as the guy who made 16 on a single hole. You don't remember? A quick recap, shot by shot:

1—It's the 2011 Valero Texas Open. Na hits his drive on the ninth hole into the woods. Na's caddy, Kenny Harms, finds it, but it's absolute jail. Kevin wants to hit it. Kenny vetoes, car or no car. "You got nothin'. Let's go back to the tee." They go back to the tee.

3—Na hits it in the *exact same place.*

Kevin: What are the odds I can get out of here?

Kenny: 50-50.

That sounds pretty good to Na.

4—Na bounces it off a branch five feet in front of him.

Kevin to Kenny: I don't know if that was a branch or if that was a ball, but something hit me.

It was the ball. One shot penalty.

6—Na hits it nowhere. Literally. They can't find it.

Kenny: Let's go back to the tee.

Kevin: Just give me another ball.

Kenny is out of vetoes. He gives him another ball.

8—Na hits it. It goes the length of a shoelace.

9, 10, 11—Na hits a small bucket in the forest. The ball keeps trying its best, but it always winds up slamming into wooden things and dropping down, exhausted. But is Na swearing, screaming, or finding a sturdy branch to hang himself? No, he's remaining in good humor.

12—The ball finally escapes the woods.

13—He hits it, but it's still not on the green.

14—It's finally on the green.

15, 16—Na two-putts for the very rare Texas Double Snowman. It is the highest score since John Daly's 18 at Bay Hill in 1998. When you have evoked a Daly disaster, that's saying something.

Still, Na is smiling. "Hey," he says. "I made a five-footer. It could've been 17."

Which brings us to the latest thing Kevin Na is known for: the Kevin Na Walk-In.

What Na does is stroke the putt and then walk briskly toward the hole to pick the ball out of it, despite the small detail that the ball hasn't stopped rolling.

"The coolest was at the [2012] US Open," Na says. "That thing was 15 feet long. I was waiting at the hole for that thing!"

But...but...but how does he know it's 100% going in? "I can tell as soon as I make contact," he says. He's been doing it since junior golf. "Especially in match play. It kinda gets to your opponent...It's a big flex."

That's true. It says to your opponent: *I'm so damn confident, I'm not going to waste your time and mine by waiting for this ball to go in the hole. I'll just snatch it out before it even stops bouncing around the bottom of the cup. This way we can both get home to supper earlier.*

OK, I know what you're thinking.

Yeah, but how stupid does he feel when he starts to walk one in and it misses?

Well, that's only happened once, on a six-footer at the 2020 Colonial, and, yes, "that was really embarrassing," he admits.

But that's the exception that proves the rule, and the rule is:

Kevin Na is a witch. He will walk a putt in anytime, anywhere. Once, on the famous par 3 island-green 17th at the TPC, Na did it from four feet out while playing with no less than Tiger Woods. Tiger watched him do it and laughed. Then he stepped up to his three-footer and walked it in Na-style, if a little less suavely. The crowd went crazy. Tiger was howling with laughter. He and Na walked off arm in arm. "I still can't believe the GOAT did that!" Na says.

Now everybody wants to be Na. Justin Bieber posted videos of him doing the Na. Also Tony Romo. Then it became a thing. People started posting doctored videos of Tiger hitting a 40-foot putt, walking over to his vanquished opponent, removing his hat, and shaking his hand—all while the ball was still rolling toward the hole.

One question: Now that Na has taught the world the walk-in putt, could somebody teach him the one-shot penalty drop?

A Beautiful Thing

There are three things that make watching a golf tournament better at home than at the actual venue: (1) the couch, (2) the beers, (3) the Toptracers.

Toptracers are the brightly colored lines that follow a shot as it rockets through the air, hooks or slices, skies or sinks. Toptracer shows you whether a shot is headed for the flagstick or the Denny's across the fence. Toptracer tells you more about a shot than the announcers ever could. A Tiger stinger on Toptracer is so cool it will cause you to spit out your tuna melt.

And to think it all started with a 26 handicapper in Sweden hitting a wedge from his snowy backyard into an empty field.

That Swede's name is Daniel Forsgren and he wears very tight pants and he is a genius. If you love a bright blue line that shows you exactly how ridiculously far Dustin Johnson just smashed it, you need to thank Daniel Forsgren.

"Because of Swedish winters, we can only play golf for maybe five months," says Forsgren, who was in his late 20s when he thought this whole idea up. "That meant the only golf we had was on TV. I loved watching it on TV, except that, as a beginner, I had no clue what I was watching. The broadcasts just show somebody hitting, the camera pointing to the sky, and then a ball landing on the green. That didn't help me at all."

Being a video gamer, Daniel was used to games with tracer fire and tracer bombs. Why couldn't they have that in golf?

Cue the light bulb.

He took a ball and his wedge and his wife out into the backyard. He gave his wife his phone and had her stand directly behind him while he hit a wedge shot out into an empty field. *(Aside to golf history buffs: That ball is still out there. Daniel never went and got it.)* Then he took that video—and here we're collapsing years and years of work, frustration, and hair-pulling into one sentence—and taught his computer to track the ball. When he finally got it, he sat back and said to nobody, "Oh my god. This is a beautiful thing!"

Exakt! as the Swedes say. Pretty soon, European Tour officials were intrigued. Collapse a bunch more years of fundraising, heartache, etc., and...they got it up and running at a tourney in Spain for a trial.

It was a complete disaster.

"The weather was terrible," Daniel recalls with a bit of a shudder. "We tracked everything but the golf ball. We tracked hail and birds and divots, but only three golf shots the entire week."

For a time in America, the best results they got were tracking festival pumpkins fired from catapults. Then there was the 2013

US Open in Merion. Steve Stricker was in the lead and Daniel's invention—then called Protracer—was bulky and awkward. "We were dragging 300 feet of cable around with us everywhere," Forsgren remembers. "We got behind Stricker in the fairway and there was noise and cable and he shanked it OB. I always felt like I cost Steve Stricker a US Open."

Now, almost a decade later, if I watch a golf tournament without Toptracer, I feel like writing a letter of grievance to somebody. Toptracer tells me so much. *Was it flighted? Did it carry on the wind? Was it a controlled draw or an unspeakable hook?* I don't have to wait for Dottie Pepper to tell me that it's headed for the flagstick; Daniel's amazing gadget has already told me.

In 2016, Forsgren's invention was purchased by Topgolf, which now uses it at its luxury golf ranges around the world (don't get me started again; see page 207). No golf broadcast worth its blazers would be without one. At the Open Championship, every shot on the practice range is Toptraced on a huge LED board for your amazement.

The skinny Swede in the tight pants is now a giant in golf. He's met nearly every great player, but his favorite is Bubba Watson—"because he hits it with SO much shape." He insists Tiger used to play with much more shape on his shots. And he pooh-poohs Rory McIlroy. "He hits it much too straight for my tastes."

Work on that, Rory.

Inherently Cool

If your dad is a famous actor, you get to be an actor. If your dad is a rich businessman, you get to be a rich businessman. But golf doesn't give a divot who your dad is.

That's what makes the story of Maverick McNealy so wonderful. Maverick is the son of billionaire software tycoon Scott McNealy, founder of Sun Microsystems. The kid could've taken his Stanford degree and started at the top. His first car could've been a Rolls. He could've chosen a career in foot-dangling.

But Maverick McNealy wanted to be a professional golfer, where the odds of making it are slightly worse than you dunking. It meant starting at the bottom, like everybody else. It meant years of Ramada Inns and KFC buckets and a whole lot of tee times with the Toro lawn mower up his butt. Here's a kid who could've topped the Tour money list without ever playing on it, yet here he is, nearly every week, trying to make a check big enough to cover his rent.

"That's one of my favorite things about golf," says McNealy, who sits perfectly erect, has the haircut of a kid going to Easter mass, and calls people "sir." "The golf ball doesn't care who you are."

His parents were all for it. But then they would be. They raised their kids to be humble. They didn't even give allowances.

Until 2021, McNealy drove his mom's 2011 Ford Explorer until the wheels nearly fell off. Yes, they lived in a mansion with its own home theater, massive pool, and hockey rink, but the four McNealy brothers all slept in one bedroom, four twin beds lined up like army barracks. "I didn't get my own room until I was a sophomore in college," McNealy says.

Sometimes, to save money, he'd have his dad caddy for him. Who knew that the 67-year-old guy in the bucket hat was one of the richest men in the world?

"He was a very, uh, invested caddy," McNealy says with a smile. "He had maybe a smaller bladder than we'd want in our caddies. A few times I was stranded in the fairway while he was in the Port-a-Potty."

OK, maybe Mr. McNealy could use Flomax, but he didn't need any help with golf. He was a +2 at one point. Mrs. McNealy shoots in the 70s still, routinely. Of course, that wasn't always the case. "My dad wouldn't propose to my mom until she could play a full 18 holes. For her first-ever full round, he made her play at the Stadium Course at PGA West, a brutal track. He counted every whiff, shank, and chunk."

What'd she shoot?

"A hundred and sixty-nine."

But here's the thing. The golf ball may not know who the McNealys are, but it definitely knows how good their son is. McNealy blew though golf's minor leagues and made his way to the PGA Tour by 23. He's played like an old salt there since. He nearly won the 2021 Pebble Beach Pro-Am.

He's a threat in every tournament he enters and his parents are loving following him around the Tour. "They have way more fun than me," Maverick says. "I'm picking up Chipotle and going back to my Residence Inn. They're staying down on Bourbon Street and having a great time."

This whole story makes my smile hurt. It takes very cool, egoless parents to bring up a kid like this. It takes an even cooler kid to take a path where the skids aren't greased. Someday Maverick McNealy will be a very rich man. Some of it might even come from his inheritance.

Life in Jupiter

It always slays me when people come up and say, "Golf is so stuffy and boring."

When I hear that, I know right away they don't know the

new golf, cool golf, music-on-the-range golf, golf-carts-with-spinning-wheels golf, finish-on-18-and-swing-off-a-rope-into-a-pond golf. Golf is so cool now, I'm amazed it's not illegal in Kansas.

Just the way you get around a course now is cool. At Coal Creek (Louisville, Colorado), you can ride a golf bike. At Monarch Beach (Dana Point, California), you can ride a kind of rolling surfboard. At Windy Knoll (Springfield, Ohio), you can ride a hovercraft.

Tour players are cooler now, too. All the fat outdoor pool sharks who needed their caddy to tie their shoes are pretty much gone. Now we've got 4-percent-fat players like Dustin Johnson, who can stand flat-footed and dunk. Collin Morikawa is so personable and bright it makes you want to have another daughter just so he could marry her. Did you know Jordan Spieth is a good piano player?

In the 1980s, all the cool could be found in only one guy—Greg Norman. He could fly a helicopter (scared me to death in it once), loved to shark dive (they swam away from him), and constantly itched to go fast, faster, fastest. I was riding in a souped-up Trans Am once with him on a rainy night in Columbus when he said, "Ready?"

For what?

Going 70 miles an hour on a slick, two-lane road, Norman threw it in neutral, yanked the steering wheel left, pulled up hard on the emergency brake, and spun a perfect 180. I saw a blur of trees and telephone poles—not to mention my life—go flying by my eyes.

When I could finally breathe again, he was laughing and yelling, "Not in the article! You can't put this in the article!"

And I didn't put it in an article. This is a book.

Jupiter, Florida, is now the official center of the New Cool. In Jupiter, Brooks Koepka doesn't live far from Justin Thomas, who sees Justin Rose around town, who waves at Matt Wolff at stoplights, who might high-five Rickie Fowler at the grocery store, who might play hoops with Keegan Bradley. They eat together, fly together, and even bowl together. You think Tiger, Ernie, and Vijay had Bowling Night?

Here's how cool golf is now: In 2021, a 27-year-old mini-tour player named Michael Visacki made a 20-footer to finally qualify for a Tour event after three years of trying. The 6-3, 300-pounder immediately called his father and wept like a child. "I made it," he told his dad. The event he got into, the Valspar in Tampa, didn't go that well, but the video went viral, which got him into the Colonial in Fort Worth, where he almost made the cut. Before he left, Justin Thomas came up and handed him a $10,000 check. "For some reason it hit home to me," Thomas explained to reporters. "It just was like, man, this is a dude who's been grinding for a long time...I just wanted to help."

Remind me. Did Lee Trevino ever do that for Orville Moody?

It's not just the players. These new courses they're building have shaken golf up like a martini. At the Cradle at Pinehurst, you can play nine of the sweetest little par 3 holes in America all day for $50. At Mike Keiser's sensational Dunes Club in New Buffalo, Michigan, there's only nine holes but eight tee boxes on each of them. You win the hole, you get to pick the next tee box. At the 22-hole Ohoopee in Georgia, some holes are par 3 1/2, some are 4 1/2. Par doesn't matter, since only match play is allowed at Ohoopee. The coasters in the bar say *Nobody Cares What You Shot*. "People go to a new course and play bad and it's,

'Aw, Gil Hanse sucks!'" says Gil Hanse, who designed Ohoopee. "But you don't keep score at Ohoopee. What matters is the fun shots you can hit."

If you want fun, play *anything* built by Discovery Land, the rope-swing people (Driftwood in Austin, Texas). At its Playa Grande course (Dominican Republic) there's a zip line that sails over the course. At Chileno Bay (Los Cabos, Mexico) they don't have beverage-cart women. They have beverage–Jet Ski women. At El Dorado (Baja coast, Mexico), you might see George Clooney and Cindy Crawford at the best taco stand you'll ever find. You make the turn to find a woman under a palapa on the beach making the most delicious morsels you've ever put in your mouth. You eat them standing up, on a surfboard, while the blue-green Pacific licks your feet. Did I mention the food is all free?

Discovery is the brainchild of Mike Meldman, whose goal in life is to turn your idea of a country club upside down. At his Gozzer Ranch (Coeur d'Alene, Idaho), where Wayne Gretzky is a member, you'll see dilapidated shacks on the course that look like Uncle Jed's house before he became a Beverly Hillbilly. My buddy once dared me to look inside one. I crept up and found... homemade jerky, deviled eggs, sliders, ribs, all the candy Veruca Salt could ever eat, and hand-churned ice cream. Did I mention the food is all free?

At any one of these Discovery deals, they can't seem to do enough for you. Whenever I'm at one, I like to play The No Game. The idea is to see if I can get any employee to say the word "no" to me.

Can I get a haircut? Sure!

Can you wash my car? Sure!

But I left it at the bar last night. Got the keys?

The only "No" I've gotten so far is from Meldman himself, when I asked:

Can I get a free membership to all your properties?

Dough Daddy

You don't meet Bob Parsons. You just try to grab on to his belt loop when he comes flying by. He's a hurricane, a force. He's everything and everything's opposite. He's a billionaire with the "dems" and "dose" of a Baltimore trucker. He's a tortured Vietnam vet who quotes Boccaccio. He's one of the most successful golf-club manufacturers in the world and yet golf treats him like a human double bogey.

He's a muscle shirt at a Newport garden party. He's about as "country club" as a Harley-Davidson. (He would know. He owns the world's largest Harley-Davidson dealership.) He wears black down to his boots and shows off his Marine Corps tattoos and yet when he goes to a black-tie fundraiser he looks at you, grins, and says, "Goddammit. Dis is gonna cost me a nudder ten mill."

He makes the most out of his life maybe because he thought he was dead at 16. He was working at a gas station when a robber came in, put a gun to his head, and was supposed to shoot him but he lost his nerve. Be glad he lived. He gives away $1 million every two weeks.

He's a savant who wants you to think he's a bouncer. He wanted to learn computer programming so he bought a book and became proficient enough to start an online accounting company. He wound up selling Parsons Technology for $64 million.

He wanted to start a domain name company, built a monster of one called GoDaddy, and wound up selling two-thirds of it for $2.25 billion.

He wanted to build a great set of golf clubs, so he stole three design engineers at Ping and told them, "Build me the best clubs ever made—and money is no object." Three years later, they delivered irons so good that people who own them want to sleep with them. His unheard-of PXG (Parsons Xtreme Golf) clubs were suddenly among the five best-selling in the country. And what's been the reaction from golf's powers that be?

Drop dead.

"I don't get why the golf world doesn't seem to give a sh*t about Bob," says PGA Tour regular Pat Perez, who plays PXGs. "Here's a guy who gives away millions every year, a guy who puts $400 million into a single golf club [Scottsdale National], a guy who starts a club company out of the blue and it's all top-of-the-line stuff, and nobody seems to talk about him. Not Golf Channel, not the world of golf, really. OK, maybe he's not golfy, but hell, a lot of us aren't golfy. Doesn't mean we don't love golf."

Oh, Parsons loves golf, but he loves it his way. Take his remarkable 45-hole Scottsdale National, where the initiation fee is $500,000. It's a kind of marble-and-velvet frat house. For instance, at Scottsdale National...

- There's no dress code. You want to play in jeans and flip-flops? Do it. The only rule is "Nobody gets to screw up anybody else's fun."
- On his Mine Shaft course, there's a bunker that's 17 feet deep and as wide as a coffin. Hit it in there and you might as well be dead. Hardly anybody ever gets it out in one. "Every time somebody does," Perez says, "Bob digs it deeper."
- When you draw your club back at his annual Wild West Invitational member-guest hootenanny, roving DJs blast train horns just to remind you your score doesn't matter. The snacks are caviar and Dom Pérignon. The women get pairs of $800 Jimmy Choos. "I spend about a mill on dat baby every year," he says.
- His Bad Little Nine par 3 track is so evil that Parsons will give $1,000 to anybody—doesn't matter whether you're Justin Thomas or Marlo Thomas—who can break par on it on a Friday, when the pins are in places a mountain goat wouldn't go. "I was playing the third hole on it once," Perez says. "I was laying 11 and still not on the green. I never did figure out how to do it."

And yet, when you consider all the things he's made and remade—GoDaddy, the PXG clubs, the billions—the most amazing thing he's remade is himself.

The son of two gamblers, Parsons volunteered for the US Marines at 17, got shipped to the front lines of Vietnam, and saw mayhem, death, and men turned inside out, literally. Once, in Quang Nam province, he stepped through a trip wire that blew him sky high. When he came to, his legs looked like raw hamburger. He reached for them with his left arm, only to be surprised to see his entire elbow bone sticking out of it.

Vietnam gave him a case of PTSD you wouldn't wish on anybody. Post-traumatic stress disorder leaves you ready to fight, under the surface, all the time. "I was always ready to be mad," Parsons says. "I didn't have any patience for nobody." If he wasn't yelling, he was sobbing. "Somebody would ask me if I served in Vietnam and I'd start crying. Pretty soon, people stop talking to you."

What finally brought him relief isn't very golfy at all—therapist-guided LSD, mushroom, ayahuasca, MDMA, and ketamine trips. Golf might spit in its lobster bisque when it reads that, but they've worked. They've rejiggered the electric synapses of his brain. He's changed. He's at peace.

"Man, I'm so much better now," he says. "You know what? I left Vietnam 48 years ago and I think I just now came home."

If golf would open its mind a little, it might see how wonderful that is.

The Man Who Ate Golf

I guess I'm supposed to hate Bryson DeChambeau, but I don't quite know why.

Fans seem to hate him because he makes golf look so ugly. He looks like Hulk swinging a tree. But have you seen how crazy far it goes?

Architects seem to hate him because he chews up their designs and spits them out. Long par 5, short par 4, dogleg? Who cares? DeChambeau plays every hole the same way—smash the dimples off it with the driver, find it in the spinach, and wedge on. It's usually good enough to beat 98% of the field, sometimes all of it.

Do you remember the setup at the 2020 US Open, on the skinny fairways of Winged Foot? The experts kept saying, "These fairways are *so* narrow, DeChambeau will *have* to hit irons off the tee." But to DeChambeau, that was the very reason he *had* to hit driver. If everybody's missing fairways, why not miss them 100 yards past everybody else? It worked. He won by six shots.

Tour players seem to hate him because he's nothing like them. He's a science nerd. He has a dozen gadgets that measure the dispersion of this and the ratio of that. He talks about "intellectual radicals" and the "bounce coefficient" of a flagstick. Drives them batty.

Here's just an abbreviated list of what DeChambeau's caddy has to do that most caddies don't:

- Spritz, heat, and freeze balls to see how it affects distance.
- Hand him his putter in a *very* particular way. "We literally had a three-minute discussion about this," says his former caddy Tim Tucker.
- Figure in air density, wind, soil type, grass type, moisture in the green, slope of the green, spin rate, launch angle, carry, run out, and total distance into every single shot. This is how Tucker, a man who flunked Algebra 3 in high

school, found himself saying: "OK, you're hitting an 8 iron with 6,900 spin. We're landing into a 2% slope on 5.4 millimeter green density, which means it's gonna run out, uh, eight yards."

"If you're going to caddy for Bryson, you're going to be the best caddy out there or you're gone," says Tucker, who now runs a luxury shuttle service at Bandon Dunes called Loop. "He's really demanding and sometimes I'd just be like, 'F*ck off!' But I really like the guy. He's a great dude and absolutely the hardest-working player I've ever seen. Not even close. He won't leave the range until he's figured it out."

One day, at the Masters, where they don't allow any of his U-Haul of gizmos, the provocateur Justin Thomas decided to tweak him a little.

Thomas: Hey, Bryson, what will you do this week?

DeChambeau: What do you mean?

Thomas: I mean, you don't have your thing that measures the moisture on the greens. How will you know the speed?

DeChambeau: Oh, well, I figured that out. I know exactly how much my caddy weighs, so I have him stand on the green and I can see how deep an impression his feet make. I measure that and then I just do the math.

This is the kind of stuff that gets you a wedgie in sixth grade.

Golf writers seem to hate him because he's "breaking the game." Me, I think he's revolutionizing it.

"I think he may have something," Jack Nicklaus says. "I wonder how long his body can hold up swinging like that, but I like him. He's got brains. The way he swings. The [locked-arm] putting. The same-length irons. Didn't Bobby Jones do that?" (Jones did and it helped him in 1930 to win the Grand Slam.)

DeChambeau is doing to golf what Dick Fosbury did to the high jump. Like Fosbury, DeChambeau's backward ways might cause sniggering now, but in five years, I guarantee a ton of players will be doing it.

Do you realize how much courage this all takes? Here's a young guy who had a great career going. He was one of only four players who'd won the NCAA Championship (SMU) and the US Amateur. He'd already won four times on Tour before all this. But he decided that wasn't good enough. He wanted to add 50 pounds to his body, change his swing entirely, and smash balls where no man had smashed them before. Eating 3,500 calories a day, he got so ridiculously big he looked like a strip-club bouncer.

What if he tried all this, with the whole world watching, and then fell flat on his face? He'd have gone down as the dumbest man in golf history. That's why he went to golf/physics coach Chris Como and said, "Help me." Como tried to tell him cautionary tales of guys who've bulked up to chase distance and lost their swing entirely. "I was nervous," Como says. "But it didn't matter. He was going to do what he wanted."

Como didn't just help him get stronger, he helped him get faster. By the fall of 2021, Beefy Bryson had added 15 yards to his drives, won a US Open and three other tournaments, and hit a drive 428 yards. At the end of the 2021 season, he was first in driving distance and top 20 in putting. Any questions?

DeChambeau has always been different. He was doing algebra at six years old. He can sign his name backward and upside down. He's a *Fortnite* freak. But different can be difficult. He wears people out.

"Bryson never does anything wrong," says one Tour caddy. "We were with him once on a drivable par 4. He had 25 yards left. He paced it off all the way to the flag, did all the rehearsal and all the math, and then he straight bladed it. He turned to his caddy and goes, 'Tim! You forgot to remind me of the elevation!' "

DeChambeau is slow, partly because he's constantly asking for rulings and then arguing when he gets rejected. He takes a Tolstoy novel to hit a putt. He shoots 70 and then goes to the range until midnight, yelling at people and breaking clubs. He craves perfection and can't understand those who don't. But wasn't Michael Jordan like that?

"People picking on him just pisses me off," Tucker says. "He'll be like, 'Tim, why are people on my ass? All I do is work my ass off on the course, then work my ass off on the range, then go home and work my ass off in the gym and then I sleep. I don't drink. I don't go to clubs. I don't get in trouble.' I think it's so unfair." Well, part of it is the way he seems to treat caddies like Tim. "It just looks that way on the internet," Tucker says. "He'll turn to me and go, 'Tim! Can you believe the way that thing snapped off at the end?' He's not yelling at me, he's just calling my attention to something. He always starts every sentence with 'Tim!' It's just a misperception."

Tour players can make fun of DeChambeau all they want, but why, when he pulls out his driver on the range, do they stop and watch? Why do they sneak over and take pictures of his Track-Man numbers and then show each other? Why is he the main subject at their dinner conversations?

Why? Because nobody's ever played the game like this kid. What's to hate?

REVOLVER

ONE DAY, I WAS *playing with the sitting US vice president, Dan Quayle, at Congressional. He was a very solid 6, with a lovely tempo and an immaculate short game. And yet...I wouldn't say he was the sharpest razor at Walgreen's.*

On one hole, he hit a long putt that looked like it was going in but stopped a millimeter short of it. I said, "Mr. Vice President, that's what we call a South American putt."

He looked at me and said, "What do you mean?"

"One more revolution," I said, grinning.

He looked at me and said, "What do you mean?"

A single golf shot has thousands of revolutions, but life only has one—one time around to live it with as much laughter and tears and discovery as we can. We all know people who think this game is a massive waste, but, me, I can't imagine my life without it. If I'd have let my resentment of my dad—my fear of winding up like him—steal golf from me, I'd have missed all of the wonderful things I've learned from it.

For one, it's taught me responsibility. Golf isn't like other sports. You didn't lose on the last hole because somebody forgot to block the linebacker or the guy had a backbreaking curve. In golf, it's on you. You put yourself in this prison. Now, can you escape it? Golf tells you exactly who you are. Did you cheat? Were you smart? When you stood over a throw-up putt, were you brave? When you failed, did you forgive yourself so you could go forward? Golf taught me that the messes I make are my fault. Not my dad's and not my 7 iron's.

For another, it's taught me humility. I remember standing with Tiger Woods at Stanford while he hit balls. In the middle of it, he stopped and said, "You know, just when I think I've figured this game out, I realize I haven't." Me, too. At 63, I shot a 66, my best ever. Each shot seemed easier than the last, every hole looked like a New York City manhole. A month later, I shot an 88. That's golf. I've won spectacularly and lost spectacularly and usually I'm not quite sure why either way. I just know I can't quit it.

It's kept me sane. Our finest living composer, John (Star Wars) Williams, once told me he has to play at least three holes at the end of every day, "Just to get the notes out of my brain. If I don't, they swim around my head all night and I can't sleep." Me, too. I write a lot of screenplays now and if I don't play golf every second or third day, the words, the stories, the characters nearly spin me into a facial tic.

Will Rogers said, "Golf is good for the soul. You get so mad at yourself you forget to hate your enemies." My buddies and I play and we soar and we sink and we alternately love and hate ourselves and have a cold beer after and laugh and wonder how we could do something that hammer-brained and when can we do it again?

Golf taught me all this, not my dad. Even after he got sober, he taught me almost nothing. Some drunks stay drunk even after the booze is gone. My dad wasn't interested as much in his wife or his kids as he was in his latest get-rich-quick scheme. Hey! I'm selling Amway now. I'm selling astronaut food! I'm selling encyclopedias, chiropractor beds, math systems! *Each scheme opened with a 77-piece marching band and a fluttering banner and ended in the gutter. My dad had a great follow-through in his golf swing, but none in life. Every scheme would be dead within six months. And all those Amway bottles and Space Sticks and encyclopedias piled up in our basement until we could barely walk around them. And then, as an adult, when he'd call me up and start telling me about his latest dig-me grandiose plan, I'd hold the phone away from my ear and grit my teeth. I became the opposite—I'd stick with an idea, a project, a relationship that was going nowhere way too long, just to keep from being like him. Maybe I should thank him for that.*

Now, years later, I realize I didn't need my dad to teach me anything. I had my brother. I had my fathers-in-law. And, yes, I had golf. Golf taught me to accept the losses as gracefully as the triumphs, and that neither of those matter as much as the trying. You shake hands and you shake it off and you try to be better next time around.

It's a stupid game that makes no sense and has taken way too big a bite out of my one revolution. And it saved me.

So Much Beauty to Hear

I like to play now and then with Tom Sullivan, the blind entertainer, just to hear all the things I've been missing.

Sullivan, sightless since birth, has lived 10 lives. He's been a singer, a pianist, a *Good Morning America* correspondent, a best-selling author, a songwriter, an after-dinner speaker, a movie star, and Johnny Carson's guest more than 50 times. He ran 22 marathons. He won 78 straight matches as a wrestler, one of them by popping out one of his artificial eyes and making his opponent puke.

But I know Tom Sullivan as my golfing buddy who loves the game as much as anybody I know, despite having never seen it. "I may be the only golfer who's never even seen the golf ball," he likes to say.

I love playing with Tom because he wakes me up. Once, he was about to hit when he suddenly stopped. "Oh, listen to that!" he said.

I looked around. "Listen to what?" I asked.

"Two starlings chasing a hawk," he said, pointing up and to the left.

Sure enough, there were two little birds up there chasing a hawk around. "Marvelous," he said.

The man is always just so *present*. He feels the wind change, he stops to feel the sun on his face, he hears conversations on other fairways. When I swing, he somehow knows whether I rushed it, flared it, or caught it pure. "I don't think I've ever seen you get through the ball like you're getting through it today," he said the other day.

OK, hold on. How do you know that?

"Well, I listen. I listen to the shaft whipping through the air and I can tell your tempo from that. Now, a fade makes a *fffffft* sound as it takes off. Whereas a hook goes *fa-fa-fa-fa*. A really good iron makes that *thump* sound. A really solid drive has that *whooosh* taking off." It struck me that I could hear those things, too, but I've never tried.

I once asked him why he took up golf in the first place.

"Because tennis would've sucked," he says with a laugh. He began learning indoors in a room his friend, former PGA Tour pro Mark Pfeil, set up for him. It had a mat and a net and a bunch of practice balls. Pfeil would teach Tom a few things, then leave him alone to work on them. Until, that is, the day when Tom "got a little turned around" and hit a perfect 5 iron right through the picture window.

Since then, Sullivan has played all over the world and with

some of the greatest players who ever lived. One day, he was playing with Jack Nicklaus, and not particularly well. After a few holes, Sullivan asked, "Jack, what do you think about my swing?"

"Well," Nicklaus said. "The best thing I can say about your golf swing is you'll never have to see it."

Nicklaus should've been there for Tom's greatest moment. It was on the 18th hole at the Sammy Davis Jr. Pro-Am near Hartford, Connecticut. The 18th is a big amphitheater of a green and there must've been 6,000 people. Now, the most dangerous part of Tom's game are the bunker shots. It's hard for him to gauge where the sand is compared to his feet, so when he steps into a bunker, you take cover. If Sullivan skulled this one, the ball was going to go 100 miles an hour straight into the massive crowd. "Tom killing somebody was definitely in play," Pfeil remembers. Fuzzy Zoeller, his partner that day, said, "Tom, why don't you pick that one up?"

"No way," Sullivan said. "I'm hitting this."

Uh-oh. Fuzzy gulped. Pfeil inhaled. The crowd braced itself, and Tom hit the most beautiful bunker shot you've ever seen, right into the hole.

Tom doesn't just eat at the buffet of life, he rides the dessert cart around the place. He does it because he wasn't sure he'd ever have any kind of life at all.

As a boy, his parents built an eight-foot-high fence around their Boston backyard so he could play without them watching him. "I remember being out there, alone, and hearing the new boy next door," he recalls. "I guess I was about eight. He was with another boy. They were playing catch. I wanted to be over there *so bad*. I thought, 'If I don't get to those boys, I'll never have a life.' So I climbed the fence—I didn't even know how high it was—got to the top, and fell all the way down. Knocked the wind out of me. I could feel the new boy, Billy Hammond, kneeling over me. He said, 'Wow. Gnarly fall.'"

That was music to Tom's ears. "Then Billy said two words that changed my life forever: 'Wanna play?'"

Sully hasn't stopped playing since.

President of What?

If there's one thing I've learned, it's that game can't be bought. It doesn't care about your portfolio, your Oscars, or your Instagram followers. Golf will give you a wedgie in front of the whole school if it wants. You can't buy a single-digit handicap with money or power or Super Bowl trophies. Golf doesn't even care if you're the most powerful man on earth. I know. I played with Bill Clinton, who was the sitting US president when we teed it up together in 1995. I wrote about it in *Sports Illustrated*, but there were a few things left out because, well...editors.

I met him at the White House and we took the presidential limo to Congressional Country Club in Bethesda, Maryland. When you are escorted by a dozen police cars and fire trucks, you make very good time. Yet, when we got there, we changed our shoes sitting on the trunk, like two muni plumbers.

Clinton was wildly into it. It was like he was getting a one-day furlough from prison and he was going to make it last as long as he could. We played for a good five hours plus. The main reason was the Billigans. A Billigan is cousin to a mulligan. It's a practice shot. Clinton would hit his first shot and then take three, four, even five extra practice shots from the same spot, trying to work out this flying elbow or that head lift. Billigans are still cheating, but more a venial sin than a mortal one. The problem with the Billigans was that, with five of his balls scattered around every hole, it was sometimes hard for Clinton to remember which one was his actual first shot. The Secret Service always seemed to go to the ball closest to the hole and say, "It's this one, Mr. President." Everybody wants to be ambassador to Sweden.

Clinton was much bigger and healthier than I expected. He hit it well, especially his irons, though his old Bulls Eye putter needed to be impeached. He shot 82-ish, which was a great day for him, and he seemed to hate to see it end. When we got back to the Oval Office to drink the cold beer he'd promised us, his desk phone was flashing like Bourbon Street.

"I'm real sorry I can't have a beer with you fellas," he apologized. "But I got this Bosnia thing breakin' out on me."

Hey, I gotta get home and fix the garage door, I thought. *Make with the Budweisers.*

After the piece came out, I was asleep on my couch in my Denver office when the phone rang. The woman on the line said, "Mr. Reilly? Please hold for the president."

And I said, groggy, "The president of what?"

There was a pause. "The United States?" she said.

Playing 18 holes with a celebrity is one of the best ways to do an interview and I've done hundreds, pro athletes especially. They tend to love golf because (1) it's a game they can't quite master and it drives them berserk, and (2) they can spend four hours without anybody wanting a picture or an autograph.

When John Elway was a Denver Broncos rookie, he was an 18 handicap. By the time he retired, he was scratch. In fact, he was, at one time, the club champion at three different Colorado clubs at the same time. Elway is great company, but when $10 is on the line, he bears down like he needs this putt to get his kids back from the terrorists. Sometimes he gets too focused. On the steep downhill 11th hole at Castle Pines one day, he hit his tee shot a little thick and took a couple steps forward, urging it to "Fly!" He didn't see the tee marker in front of him and tripped, which sent him tumbling down the hill, clear to the next set of tee boxes. He must've fallen for 10 full seconds. I laughed so hard I could barely get the tee in the ground.

Olympic figure skater Scott Hamilton is married with kids, but he's a male ice skater, so a lot of people automatically assume he's gay. He loves that. He'd crank a long drive, turn to me, and say, "Do you realize you just got outdriven by a man who wears sequins?"

Hockey players are all about the team. Playing with Wayne Gretzky in a scramble once, we came to the long drive hole and I uncorked a monster (for me). Still, it came up five yards short of the long drive sign. "Damn," I said, "almost." Gretzky shook his head and said, "What are you talking about?" Then he picked up the sign, walked back to my ball, wrote my name on the sign, and planted it there.

Weeks after O. J. Simpson was found innocent in his criminal trial, I went to LA to find him. I knew he'd been kicked out of Riviera and heard he was just bumming around the LA munis, working his way into games as a single. (Imagine that.) My photog and I found him at the turn at Rancho Park, one of the busiest munis in the city. I'd met him a few times and he seemed to remember me.

"You mind if I walk the back nine and ask you a few questions?"

He glared for a moment. "OK, but only golf questions," he said sternly. "No questions about The Incident."

"Absolutely, golf questions only," I said.

So off we went. My first question was: "Now, Juice, has your backswing changed since you killed those two people?"

OK, that's not true.

Simpson was a good player, maybe a high single digit, and, ironically, a strict rules freak. He putted everything out. He wore a black Callaway golf shirt that day and at the end of the round, he asked if we were going to run a picture of him in it.

"Sure," I said, curious. "Why?"

"Well, I used to be on Callaway's freebie list," he said, "but I notice since The Incident, I don't seem to be getting the stuff anymore. Thought it might help."

I was thinking about that later. You're at the Callaway board of directors meeting and the chairman says, *Do you realize that we don't have a single double murderer on our freebie list? Let's get on it, people!*

I guess my favorite celebrities to play with are sports announcers, because they never stop being sports announcers. Bob Costas will actually do play-by-play of his own swing. One time, he stood over it, drew it back, and said, "A little over the top for Costas and that's NOT gonna be good [*whack*] and... [looking up] indeed it is NOT good! A big banana slice for the young St. Louis native. NOT what he had in mind."

I was sitting at a lunch table with Vin Scully once and asked him about a recent hole in one he'd made. Suddenly, he launched into that wonderful maple-syrup storyteller we all love so much. "Well, it's funny," he began. "I was playing with a guy who'd make a cup of COFFEE nervous, so I wasn't really enjoying the round all that much. Well, we get to the fifth hole and I hit a shot that sounded like I'd hit it with the morning paper. You'd figure it wasn't going to make it to the green. But, as it turns out, I'd also hit the wrong club, so, lo and behold, it flew straight at the pin and—whaddya know?—it went straight into the hole!" I was sure he was then going to add, "And that story brought to you by Farmer John..."

Playing with Al Michaels is fascinating. I once asked him about the incredible staying power of his "Do you believe in miracles?" call at the 1980 US Olympics. He said, "It's amazing how long it's lasted. Some people think it was canned, like I'd taped it beforehand. If they only knew how little time we had. It was absolutely off the cuff." Michaels is just a natural-born play-by-play guy. He can't turn it off. I found that out later in the round, when I hit a 9 iron straight over the pin on a 152-yard par 3. It landed on the back fringe, then started trickling slowly back toward the pin. Michaels instantly launched into announcer mode. "Hold on, folks," he said, "we're not done yet. This might be...It could be...IT IS! AN ACE FOR REILLY!"

Greatest moment of my life.

The Egg Man

You know how wives are. All they want to do is play golf with their pals, every single day. So what are husbands supposed to do?

For RJ Smith of Rochester, Minnesota, there was only one

solution: go to the course *with* her. Not to hit golf balls. To hunt for them.

"That way my wife always knew where I was at," RJ liked to tell friends. "I wadn't sittin' at the bar someplace, drinkin'."

You always knew where RJ and Dee were—together. They were inseparable teenage sweethearts. RJ went off at 17 with the Marines to fight World War II, came right back, and married her. He became a cement finisher, carpet installer, and eventually had his own carpet and tile store. Dee gave him five children— three daughters and two sons. They loved and laughed and, when two of the daughters died, grieved.

When RJ retired, he wanted to be as close to Dee as he could, but he didn't much like playing golf. "I couldn't get her off the golf course and she couldn't get me on." He'd caddied as a kid and knew his way around the game, so he started beating the woods for balls. He had a knack for it. He'd bring them back to the little barn behind their house and organize them. Pretty soon, he was obsessed.

"He'd come into the shop," says Northern Hills head pro Mike Manahan, "and he'd say, 'I'm goin' to the office. Hold all my messages, will ya?'" Didn't matter whether it was raining or blowing or burning down hot, if Dee was out there, RJ was out there. He was unstoppable. He'd wear jeans and sneakers, come back dripping in sweat with burrs in his hair, thistles in his socks, and the day's catch in his bag. A slow day would be 10 balls, a big day would be 50. He liked it even better than fishing. Every nibble landed.

He began collections. He had every NFL team ball, every Super Bowl ball, every car manufacturer ball. He became a golf ball expert. He didn't just have one of every *brand* ever made.

And he didn't just have one of every *kind* of every brand ever made. He had one from every *year* of every *kind* of every ball ever made. He had balls back as far as 1917. You know you're good at finding balls when you find ones that were hit during WWI.

When Dee was finished with her game, she'd come find him and he'd take his bounty back to the barn. If it was a ball he already had, he'd give it away. He gave away thousands. A ball that fit into a collection would go into a 64-count cardboard egg tray. Those egg trays were stacked seven trays high and went into big plastic milk crates. Those milk crates were stacked in the barn, floor to ceiling. Eventually, RJ Smith had over 70,000 balls, no two alike.

But when his Dee died in 2002, RJ was a little lost. "You always hope you'll go first but it don't always work that way," he once said. He didn't really know what to do with himself. So like a dog that keeps walking to the gate to look for his dead master, RJ just kept going to the golf course. The kids put a memorial bench by the third green for her, so RJ would sit out there, seven mornings a week, and talk to her. When he was done, he'd go to the clubhouse, get a cart, and get back to the hunt.

All those egg crates of balls were eventually sold at auction with every dime going to charity.

Sixteen years after Dee passed, RJ Smith died of cancer at 90 years old.

Now they know where each other are.

The Payoff

Nobody loves golf more than Lenny (Two Down) O'Connor, who is (maybe I've mentioned?) the World's Most Avid Golf Gambler. The only problem is golf never loves him back. It slaps him around, keys his car, and takes his lunch money. And yet Two Down is as optimistic as a six-year-old waking up on Christmas.

One day, when he was 53, he stood up from the post-round Budweisers with the Usuals and crowed, "I guarantee, you bastards! Someday, before I die, I'll be a single digit. Mark my words!"

This caused my eyebrows to go up half an inch. "Bet?" I asked.

"Excuse me?" he said, leaning in, cupping his ear and arching his over-caffeinated eyebrows.

"Bet me," I declared.

"Bet you what?"

"Hundred bucks says you won't be a single digit before you die."

That caused the table to go crazy and Two Down to throw his arms up. He frantically adjusted his glasses and his gravity-defying haircut and looked around the room as if he needed witnesses.

"Are you saying you DON'T think I'll be a single digit at least once in my life?"

"Correct," I said.

I knew this was catnip for Two Down, who was a 17 then. I

knew because of the bet he made one time with Simon the Likable. Simon was our cheery, ruddy-cheeked, blue-eyed buddy. Simon was so likable that he had to figure in extra time to get anywhere, accounting for all the people who wanted to stop and hug him. Simon was a 12. Two Down made a bet that called for Simon to only have to give him one shot a side, lifetime, no matter how good or awful each of them got. Even if Two Down lost all his toes in a lawn-mower accident, he only got one a side. I believe Simon redid his basement on that bet.

That was in my head when I repeated: "Hundred bucks. Never gonna happen."

"You're on!" he bellowed and then began ricocheting around the bar for a while. Next thing I knew, his hand was in front of me, ready to shake.

Uh-oh. Eagerness to bet. A Two Down warning sign. What had I missed?

"Wait a minute!" I said, pulling my hand back. "How do I get paid? You could be 90 years old and still think you're gonna be a single digit!"

That was very true. Two Down wouldn't give it up even if he had no legs left. "I won't be able to collect the hundo until you're dead," I said. "Then it's too late. No bet."

The Usuals agreed this was a problem.

"I tell you what," Two said soberly. "I'll tell Jane-o (his long-suffering wife) that I have to be buried in my blue blazer. She knows the one. With the brass buttons. I'll insist she bury me in that. I'll stick a $100 bill in the inside pocket. She won't know. Then, at the funeral, you reach in there and pull it out."

"What?" I protested. "I can't just reach into a coffin and take money out of a dead guy's jacket!"

"No, no, no!" Two insisted. "You come up to the altar all weepy to say your last goodbyes. You see me lying there. Then you collapse in grief and throw yourself over the coffin, sobbing. While you're over me, you secretly reach in and get the hundred."

I stroked my chin.

"Could work," I said. "No cremations?"

"No cremations."

"Blue blazer?"

"Still fits."

"How do you know Jane-o won't pilfer the hundred?" Sunshine interjected.

"Why would she?" Two countered. "She doesn't know it's in there!"

"What if the dry cleaner pockets it?" said Simon.

"I'll get it cleaned tomorrow, then I'll put the hundred in. It'll still be in plastic."

I couldn't see any more trapdoors.

"Bank," I said.

The Usuals oohed and aahed. We shook hands. Two Down bounced back from the handshake like it was an electric wire. "Easiest hundred I ever made!"

But I knew the truth. It was like a balding man hoping his hairline would suddenly go in reverse.

Twenty years later . . .

I met Two Down for lunch at his usual steak-joint corner table. Two always insisted on a seat in the corner so nobody could come up on him from behind. He had some years in Chicago that

"I just can't talk about." He was 73 and his handicap was 26. Like the national debt, it had only gone up.

And yet the first thing he said was, "Riles! My swing is really coming around. You should see it. Smooth! That hundred is as good as mine!"

But I wasn't there to talk about the bet. I wanted to talk about Simon the Likable. He was dying.

We'd noticed it a few months before. He and Two Down had come to LA for a three-day golf-dice-laughfest. Simon wasn't himself. He showed up for the first round in jeans. You can't play a country club in jeans.

"Simon, you going to a rodeo?" I asked.

"What?" he said, looking at his pants.

The next morning, Simon asked, "How much money you think I'll need today?"

"Well," I said, "you got the caddy tip, maybe something for Manny, the locker room guy, something for the valet. Maybe $200?"

He looked crestfallen. He opened his wallet to show that he only had $20.

"Is this enough?"

Two and I looked at each other. What was going on?

On the last day, we were playing the 17th hole only to find Simon on the 13th. He'd wandered into another group entirely.

A week later, Two Down called me. "Simon has early-onset dementia," he said. "They're gonna put him in a home."

Simon died four years later. That shook me. He was only three years older than me. It was the first time I realized that all this wall-to-wall golf fun could actually end.

I wasn't afraid of dying. I'd had plenty of everything—hits and flops, brilliance and stupidity, fulfillment and emptiness. I'd seen everything, twice. I could let go. It was just that, for the first time, it hit me I didn't have forever to say all the things I wanted to say to the people I loved.

That's when I started writing this book, my little thank you to the game and its people. That's also when I made up my mind to tell everybody—my family, my buddies, my colleagues—how grateful I felt.

That day, as Two Down and I were getting up from the table, I put my hands on his shoulders. "Two," I said. "I really came here just to tell you how much fun you've made golf for me."

He tried to brush me off, but I held on tighter.

"I'm serious. Your crazy schemes and your bets and all your madness, they opened my eyes to how hilarious life can be."

My eyes were starting to well up but I didn't stop to wipe them. "I'm serious. I want you to know how lucky I feel that you've been in my life. It's been a blast, buddy."

Two Down stared at me.

"Aww, same here, Riles," he said. "But you're still not getting the hundred early."

Major Gift

When you cover the majors for a living, the people you meet go a little bonkers. "Oh my god!" they gush. "Could you bring me a Masters sweater?" "Do you get to eat dinner with Phil?" "Do you get to play the courses after?"

(Answers: Yes. Definitely not. Sometimes.)

But the problem with going to nearly every major for 30-plus years is that you never get to just sit and watch them. Not with a frosty, and not with your buddies and not with your kids.

But my buddy Duncan did. For the last four years of his dad's life, Duncan Brantley would fly from LA to Charlotte, then drive to Greensboro, North Carolina, to watch the four majors in the friendly confines of an assisted living home.

It was the best gift Duncan could've given his dad. See, fathers don't want sons to know they're lonely. They don't want sons to feel sorry for them. They get itchy if things start feeling like a Red Cross visit. That's what makes golf on TV so perfect. In between Tiger Miracle Saves and Phil Is Being Held Captive by Trees dramas, you can sneak in harmless little questions like, "So how you feeling, Pops?" and "Remember Mom's spaghetti casserole?"

Besides, Jack Brantley loved golf the way puppies love slippers. He played on the University of North Carolina golf team, with the great Harvie Ward, and competed in tournaments, at scratch, all over the South. When you love golf, it doesn't end just because you can't play it anymore.

Duncan would arrive on Wednesday night and by Thursday morning, he'd be plunked down on his dad's couch, ready to watch every single shot with the man who cut down his first set of clubs. They'd comment on all the shots, all the glories, and all the failures, all fueled by Carolina BBQ and hush puppies and whatever else Duncan could order up to avoid the mush of the cafeteria.

"Dad was a southern man of style," Duncan remembers. "So his favorite player was Adam Scott, because of how great he looked on the course. And Webb Simpson, because he was polite and from Charlotte. I mean, he'd take a Tiger win, but he really pulled for those two."

Duncan never missed a single major, even though it meant sandwiching himself into seat 27A on Southwest from LA to Charlotte four times a year, five in Ryder Cup years. "Those visits," he says with a little sigh, "were fantastic. Golf truly was the thing that brought him the most joy. My relationship with my dad in the last four years was as good as it ever was in our lives."

Hearing about Duncan and his dad always made me ache a little about my dad, who was also called Jack. I was always *at* those tournaments, so I never got to watch them with him. Even when I'd take him to majors, I couldn't walk with him. I had to work. When he got too old to travel, I'd call him from the press room and tell him stories—"My phone went off right on Tiger's backswing!"—but it was all kind of lost through the phone lines and the hearing aids.

As the years mounted and Jack Brantley's dementia began inching deeper, he couldn't follow the day's storyline—*Tiger is trying to catch Molinari; Spieth is losing his lead*—but it didn't matter. He could understand each shot as it came. *Dustin Johnson is trying to cut it around this tree.* Jack could understand that. He used to have that shot. And when Johnson would pull it off, he'd smile. *Well done, young man.*

On the last visit, the last putt dropped. CBS interviewed the teary winner and that was that. Duncan shut the TV off and started talking about leaving. Seat 27A was calling.

Jack Brantley stared at the TV for a bit, looked at his old hands, and then looked at his son.

"We gonna watch the golf?" he asked.

Duncan looked at him, smiled, and said, "Well, of course, Dad."

Then he plunked himself back down, turned the TV back on, switched to the Golf Channel replay, and watched it all over again.

GRANDFATHER

I WAS FRIENDS WITH the late songwriter Mac Davis. He wrote "In the Ghetto" for Elvis and only a few dozen other monster hits. Had his own variety show on CBS. Opened for Sinatra.

He was a music machine. I'd say something odd and he'd turn the phrase into a country song, just like that, right in the middle of the fairway. But when he turned 70, it all started coming unglued. His eyes got floating black dots in front of them and his body started to cave in and everything hurt. One day, he said, "Riles, don't wait till it's too late. Get it while you can." He was gone from us at 78.

That's one reason I retired early. The other reason was the day my son Jake got me on a Zoom and told me he and his wife, Aimee, were expecting. Surprise. It would be my first grandchild. I don't know why, but I wept. There was something so complete about that moment, like whatever part I had played in my kids' lives was done and they could take it from here and there was nothing left for me but to bite into as much of the world as I could before I couldn't chew solids anymore.

I knew little Elio was a true Reilly at one year old, when I was babysitting. He started teeing up plastic golf balls and whacking them so hard that they'd bounce off the ceiling, then the fridge, then the dining room table, then me. I'd grab the ball, do a double take at it, then back at him, then back at the ball. He'd double over laughing and start to tee up another one.

I looked at his perfect little face and thought of how he'd never have to be afraid of his dad, how he could be a regular kid, not a fight referee. And I said, "Kid, you're gonna have so much fun with this game, you're gonna wish you were twins."

———————